D0816089

GOOGLE
Pocket Guide

GOOGLE
Pocket Guide

*Tara Calishain, Rael Dornfest,
and DJ Adams*

O'REILLY®

Beijing · Cambridge · Farnham · Köln · Paris · Sebastopol · Taipei · Tokyo

Google Pocket Guide
by Tara Calishain, Rael Dornfest, and DJ Adams

Published by O'Reilly & Associates, Inc., 1005 Gravenstein Highway North, Sebastopol, CA 95472.

O'Reilly & Associates books may be purchased for educational, business, or sales promotional use. Online editions are also available for most titles (*safari.oreilly.com*). For more information, contact our corporate/institutional sales department: (800) 998-9938 or *corporate@oreilly.com*.

Editor:	Rael Dornfest
Production Editor:	Colleen Gorman
Cover Designer:	Edie Freedman
Interior Designer:	David Futato

Printing History:

June 2003:	First Edition.

0-596-00550-4
[C]   [12/03]

Contents

Part V. Appendix

Google Pocket Guide

Introduction

The success of Google™ in becoming the search engine for everybody is phenomenal and not to be ignored. Google's simplicity, exemplified by its visual presence on the Web, is skin deep: have you ever stopped to wonder what sort of engine lies beneath the surface of that serene front page, the engine that continues to amaze and astound those that ask it to find things for them? When Google first came onto the search scene, we marveled at how it seemed to instinctively know just what we were looking for. Today, people take that for granted; because Google "just works," it's easy to forget the incredible power of that engine.

It's likely that you've used Google already to find things on the Web. And it's probably helped you do just that. This book is about getting the most from Google's underlying power—understanding how to be more precise in telling it what you're looking for, by learning about how to get the most out of your search keywords, discovering and bringing to bear the somewhat undocumented special syntax that Google offers, and helping Google find what you're looking for.

Furthermore, Google is more than just a search engine. There are plenty of offerings within and around Google to help you get to what you want—language tools, newsgroup article searching, search toolbars, image searches, and much more.

Here's a quick rundown of what you'll find in this book:

Part I, *What Can You Do with Google?*
Part I gives you an overview of Google's features and facets. We look at what Google is and what Google isn't, and start off simple, offering a few case studies to inspire you.

Part II, *Asking for What You Want*
In Part II, you learn how to construct search queries, making the most of Google's special syntax and advanced search features. You also learn how to work around some of the restrictions that Google places on search criteria.

Part III, *Understanding What You Get*
There's more to Google's search results than one might expect. Part III helps you understand what those results mean and how to get the most from the information you're handed.

Part IV, *Other Google Services and Features*
There are plenty of things that Google offers that you might not be aware of. Looking for phone numbers, stock information, news, images, or catalog contents? Part IV shows you how to use Google to find this stuff and much more.

Part V, *Appendix*
Part V contains two reference sections: a syntax summary and a discussion of Julian dates.

If this book whets your appetite for more information, check out its big sibling, *Google Hacks* (*http://www.oreilly.com/ catalog/googlehks/*), a collection of industrial-strength, real-world, tested solutions to problems solvable with Google.

Conventions Used in This Book

The following typographical conventions are used in this book:

Italic

> Indicates new terms, URLs, web sites, filenames, file extensions, pathnames, and directories.

`Constant width`

> Shows text that should be typed literally, as well as Google-specific syntax keywords, the contents of files, or the output from commands.

`Constant width italic`

> Shows typed text that should be replaced with user-supplied values.

Menus/Navigation

> Menus and their options are referred to in the text as File → Open, Edit → Copy, etc.

↵

> Appears at inserted linebreaks; indicates the continuation of a line in a URL or in code.

NOTE

Indicates a tip, suggestion, or general note.

WARNING

Indicates a warning or caution.

PART I

What Can You Do with Google?

If you've picked up this book, it's almost certain that you know what Google is, and you want to learn more about how to ask Google for what you want and how to understand what Google returns to you in response. If so, this is just the book for you.

But before we start, it's worth examining what Google is and what Google isn't.

What Google Isn't

The Internet is not a library. The library metaphor presupposes so many things—a central source for resource information, a paid staff dutifully indexing new material as it comes in, a well-understood and rigorously adhered-to ontology—that trying to think of the Internet as a library can be misleading.

Let's take a moment to dispel some of these myths right up front.

Google's index is a snapshot of everything online. No search engine—not even Google—knows everything. There's simply too much and it's all flowing too fast to keep up. Then there's the content Google notices but chooses not to index at all: movies, audio, Flash animations, and innumerable specialty data formats.

Everything on the Web is credible. It's not. There are things on the Internet that are biased, distorted, or just plain wrong—whether intentional or not. Visit the Urban

Legends Reference Pages (*http://www.snopes.com*) for a taste of the kinds of urban legends and other misinformation making the rounds of the Internet.

Content filtering protects you from offensive material. While Google's optional content filtering is good, it's certainly not perfect. You may well come across an offending item among your search results.

Google's index is a static snapshot of the Web. It simply can't be so. The index, as with the Web itself, is always in flux. A perpetual stream of spiders deliver newfound pages, note changes, and inform of pages now gone. And the Google methodology itself changes as its designers and maintainers learn. Don't get into a rut of searching a particular way; to do so is to deprive yourself of the benefit of Google's evolution.

What Google Is

Generally speaking, there are two types of search engines on the Internet. The first is the *searchable subject index*. This kind of search engine searches only the titles and descriptions of sites, and doesn't search individual pages. Yahoo! is a searchable subject index. Then there's the *full-text search engine*, which uses computerized "spiders" to index millions, sometimes billions, of pages. These pages can be searched by title or content, allowing for much narrower searches than a searchable subject index. Google is a full-text search engine.

The way most people use an Internet search engine is to drop in a couple of keywords and see what turns up. While in certain domains that can yield some decent results, it's becoming less and less effective as the Internet gets larger and larger.

To that end, Google provides some special syntax elements (also referred to as *advanced search operators*) to help its engine understand what you're looking for. Part II takes a detailed look at Google's syntax and how best to use it to guide Google in finding what you're looking for. Briefly:

Within the page
> Google supports syntax that allows you to restrict your search to certain components of a page, such as the title or the URL.

Kinds of pages
> Google allows you to restrict your search to certain kinds of pages, such as educational sites (those ending in *.edu*) or pages that were indexed within a particular period of time.

Kinds of content
> Google can sift through results for particular file types—Microsoft Word documents, Excel spreadsheets, and PDF files, for instance. You can even find specialty web pages the likes of XML, SHTML, or RSS.

Special collections
> Google has several more specialized search properties, but some of them aren't as removed from the web index as you might think. You may be aware of Google's index of news stories and images, but do you know about Google's university searches? Or how about the special searches that allow you to restrict your searches by topic, to BSD, Linux, Apple, Microsoft, or the U.S. government?

These special syntax elements are not mutually exclusive. On the contrary, it's in the combinations that the true magic of Google lies. Search for certain kinds of pages in special collections or specific page elements in particular types of pages.

If you get one thing out of this book, get this: the possibilities are (almost) endless. This book can teach you techniques, but if you just learn them by rote and then never apply them, they won't do you any good. Experiment. Play. Keep your search requirements in mind and try to bend the resources provided in this book to your needs—build a tool-box of search techniques that works specifically for you.

A Simple Example

Let's find our bearings with a straightforward search example. Google's front page (shown in Figure 1) is deceptively simple: a search form consisting of a single text field and a couple of buttons. Yet that basic interface—so alluring in its simplicity—belies the power of the Google engine underneath and the wealth of information at its disposal. And if you use Google's search syntax to its fullest, the Web is your research oyster.

Figure 1. Google's front page

What's on the front page?

For a start, there's the search-keyword input box. In here go not only the keywords you're telling Google to look for, but also the special syntax mentioned earlier and explained in Part II.

Alongside are links to more advanced search functionality offered by Google:

Advanced Search

The Google Advanced Search goes well beyond the capabilities of the default simple search, providing a powerful fill-in form for date searching, filtering, and more. We'll look at the features of Advanced Search in Part II.

Preferences

Google's preferences provide a nice, easy way to set your searching preferences from this moment forward. We'll show you how in Part III's "Setting Preferences."

Language Tools

In the early days of the Web, it seemed like most web pages were in English. But as more and more countries have come online, materials have become available in a variety of languages—including languages, such as Esperanto and Klingon, which don't originate with a particular country.

Google offers several language tools, including one for translation and one for Google's interface. The interface option is much more extensive than the translation option, but the translation has a lot to offer. Part IV shows how to use these language tools, along with other services and features.

Along the top, there are tabs linking beyond the default Web search to additional Google services:

Images

Google Images (*http://images.google.com*) offers an archive of over 400 million images culled from sites all over the Web. Images range in size (from icon to wallpaper) and content (from portraits to logos to maps), with a variety of search options for homing in on the most appropriate.

Groups

Usenet is a global network of discussion groups. Google Groups (*http://groups.google.com*) has archived Usenet discussions as far back as 20 years, providing an archive of over 700 million messages.

Directory

The Google Directory (*http://directory.google.com*) is a searchable subject index based on the Open Directory Project (*http://www.dmoz.org*). As it indexes sites (not pages), it's much smaller than the Web search but better for general searches. Google has applied its popularity algorithm to the listings so that more popular sites rise to the top, creating a truly best-of-mixed-breed subject/full-text index.

News

Google News (*http://news.google.com*) continuously mines over 4,500 news sources for breaking news and the freshest of events. Headlines are clustered by subject, affording a nice overview of the headline at hand from a variety of points of view.

We'll explore these offerings, and more that do not yet have their own tab on the front page, in Part IV.

Now for a quick look at a typical results page, as shown in Figure 2.

You'd think a list of search results would be pretty straight-forward, wouldn't you—just a page title and a link, possibly a summary? Not so with Google. Google encompasses so many search properties and has so much data at its disposal that it fills every results page to the rafters. Within a typical search result, you can find sponsored links, ads, links to stock quotes, page sizes, spelling suggestions, and more.

Part III explains how to interpret Google's results pages and URLs, and set preferences to influence what those pages contain.

Figure 2. A typical Google results page

Improving Your Google Results

Let's finish this part of the book with a look at a few examples of where a little knowledge of Google's search facilities goes a long way to improving your search lot. Knowing how to be specific with your search criteria is key. That's what this book is all about.

Case A: Joseph Lomax, Student

Joseph is using the Web to research a history project in class. He needs to find out all he can about Julius Caesar. Naturally, his first attempt is to simply try:

```
caeser
```

Yes, we know that's not the correct spelling of Caesar, and so does Google.

As is its wont, Google tries its utmost to give Joseph what he asked for, returning links to the web site of rock and roll band, "Caeser Pink," and a misspelled online copy of "The Life and Death of Julies Caeser [*sic*]."

Google also helpfully suggests the correct spelling, as shown in Figure 3.

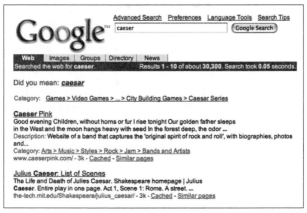

Figure 3. Google suggests the proper spelling of Caesar

By clicking on the hyperlinked correct spelling of "caesar," Joseph is back on track.

Google responds with a set of results that are almost, but not quite, what he might have expected. While the first couple of hits—"Julius Caesar: The Last Dictator" and "The Julius Caesar Site"—are spot on, the rest of the results page is peppered with various and sundry hits that are not: the Center of Advanced European Studies and Research (CAESAR), the Dutch guitar pop band Caesar, Corporate Information Employment Opportunities Investor Relations Responsible, and of course Caesar's in Las Vegas.

Unperturbed, he applies a little knowledge of Google's special syntax and tries again:

```
caesar site:edu
```

Bingo! By telling Google to restrict the search for his keyword to educational institutions (web sites whose URLs end in *.edu*), the proportion of relevant hits on the first page is vastly improved. Joseph can now start digging into the sites that Google found for him.

Case B: Sabine Reitz, Journalist

Sabine has been tasked with finding out about what people have been saying recently about ERP software company SAP's NetWeaver platform. She's writing an article for a German business magazine and wants Google to find her German-language online content.

Realizing she's going to need more than a simple keyword search, she visits Google's Advanced Search page (*http://www.google.com/advanced_search*). She specifies her search terms:

```
SAP NetWeaver
```

Since she wants only pages written in German, she specifies so using the Language pull-down list. Being a journalist, she's interested in only the freshest of content, so she asks only for content indexed by Google in the past three months. Finally, she's pretty sure that what she's looking for will turn up in the first couple of pages, so she sets the number of search results shown on a page to 20, rather than have the default of 10. Sabine's Advanced Search resembles the page shown in Figure 4.

Google returns her about 3,000 results, and indeed the most relevant all turn out to be linked from the first page of results.

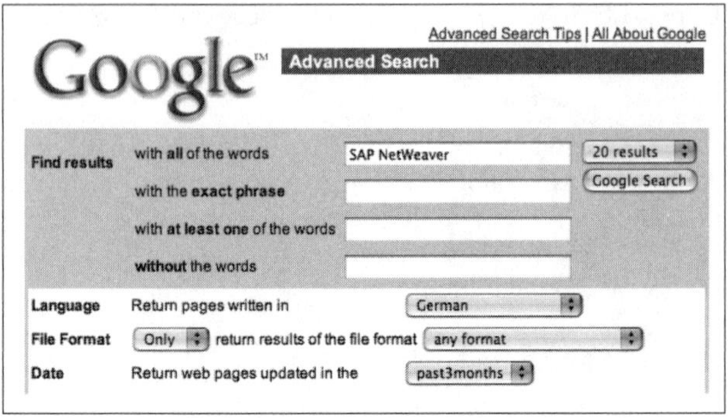

Figure 4. An Advanced Search for fresh, German "SAP NetWeaver" content

Drilling a bit deeper, she would like to see if any of those results were in Microsoft PowerPoint format, so she adds:

```
filetype:ppt
```

to the search terms displayed in the input box at the top of the results page, and hits Enter again. She actually could have done this on the Advanced Search page using the File Format pull-down list, but she's familiar with Google's special syntax and takes a shortcut.

Sabine's result—there's only one, and it's just what she's looking for, too—is shown in Figure 5.

Figure 5. Results for fresh, German "SAP NetWeaver" content in PowerPoint format

Case C: Dr. Katie Aston, Dentist

Dr. Aston is trying to find associations of dental practitioners. Armed with a little bit of knowledge—the URL of the British Dental Association (BDA)—she asks Google to give her a list of pages related to the BDA:

```
related:www.bda-dentistry.org.uk
```

Google duly obliges, listing 25 different web sites. Noticing that Google has returned a Category value for each site, she chooses one that catches her eye—Health > Dentistry > Associations—and follows the link. It's a node in the Google Web Directory (see Figure 6), and it contains a fountain of links to dental associations. Job done.

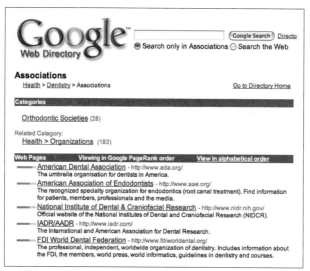

Figure 6. Related sites in the Google Web Directory

If you can combine a little bit of knowledge about what you're looking for with a good grasp of what Google has to offer, then you're on your way to great search experiences and germane results with Google. While simply throwing your search terms at Google has an uncanny habit of finding you pretty much what you want, why not harness the power of the engine beneath to dig deeper and explore still further?

PART II

Asking for What You Want

Searching in Google doesn't have to be a case of just entering what you're looking for in the search box and hoping for
the best. Google offers you many ways—via special syntax
and search options—to refine your search criteria and help
Google understand better what it is you're looking for. In
this part of the book, we'll dig into Google's powerful, all-
but-undocumented special syntax and search options, and
show how to use them to their fullest. We'll cover the basics
of Google searching, wildcards, word limits, syntax for special cases, mixing syntax elements, advanced search techniques, and using specialized vocabularies including slang
and jargon.

Google Basics

Whenever you search for more than one keyword at a time, a
search engine has a default strategy when it comes to han-
dling and combining those keywords. Can those words
appear individually anywhere in a page, or do they have to be
right next to each other? Will the engine search for both keywords or for either keyword?

Phrase Searches

Google defaults to searching for occurrences of your specified
keywords anywhere in the page, whether side-by-side or scat-
tered throughout. If you specifically want words to appear
together on a page for a match to be made, let Google know

by enclosing them in quotes, turning your keyword search into a *phrase search*, to use Google's terminology.

On entering a search for the keywords:

```
to be or not to be
```

Google will find matches where the keywords appear any-where on the page. If you want Google to find you matches where the keywords appear together as a phrase, surround them with quotes, like this:

```
"to be or not to be"
```

Google will return matches only where those words appear together. (Not to mention explicitly including stop words like "to" and "or"; see the section "Explicit Inclusion" a lit-tle later.)

Phrase searches are also useful when you want to find a phrase but aren't quite sure of the exact wording. This is accomplished in combination with wildcards, explained later in "Full-Word Wildcards."

Basic Boolean

As to whether the engine searches for all keywords or any of them, the answer is called a Boolean default; search engines can default to Boolean AND (it'll search for all of your key-words) or Boolean OR (it'll search for any of your keywords). Of course, even if a search engine defaults to searching for all keywords, you can usually give it a special command to instruct it to search for any keyword. But the engine has to know what to do if you don't give it instructions.

Google's Boolean default is AND; that means if you enter query words without modifiers, Google will search for all of your query words. For example, if you search for:

```
snowblower Honda "Green Bay"
```

Google will search for all the words. If you prefer to specify that any one word or phrase is acceptable, put an OR between each:

```
snowblower OR snowmobile OR "Green Bay"
```

If you particularly want one term along with one of two or more other terms, group them with parentheses, like so:

```
snowblower (snowmobile OR "Green Bay")
```

This query searches for the word "snowmobile" or phrase "Green Bay" along with the word "snowblower." A stand-in for OR borrowed from the computer programming realm is the | (pipe) character, as in:

```
snowblower (snowmobile | "Green Bay")
```

Negation

If you want to specify that a query item must *not* appear in your results, prepend a – (minus sign or dash):

```
snowblower snowmobile -"Green Bay"
```

This will search for pages that contain both the words "snowblower" *and* "snowmobile," but *not* the phrase "Green Bay."

Note that the – symbol must appear directly before the word or phrase you don't want. If there's space between, as in the following query, it won't work as expected:

```
snowblower snowmobile - "Green Bay"
```

Do be sure, however, that there's a space before the – symbol.

Explicit Inclusion

On the whole, Google will search for all the keywords and phrases you specify (with the exception of those you've specifically negated with –, of course). However, there are certain words that Google will ignore, words that are so common that they generally won't help in the search. These words—"I," "a," "the," and "of," to name a few—are called *stop words*.

You can force Google to take a stop word into account by prepending a + (plus) character, as in:

```
+the king
```

Stop words that appear inside of phrase searches are not ignored. Searching for:

```
"the move" glam
```

will result in a more accurate list of matches than:

```
the move glam
```

simply because Google takes the word "the" into account in the first example but ignores it in the second.

Simple Searching and Feeling Lucky

The I'm Feeling Lucky™ button is a thing of beauty. Rather than giving you a list of search results from which to choose, you're whisked away to what Google believes is the most relevant page given your search (i.e., the first result in the list). Entering washington post and clicking the I'm Feeling Lucky button takes you directly to *http://www.washingtonpost.com*. Trying president will land you at *http://www.whitehouse.gov*.

Case Sensitivity

Some search engines are case-sensitive; that is, they search for queries based on how the queries are capitalized. A search for "GEORGE WASHINGTON" on such a search engine would not find "George Washington," "george washington," or any other case combination.

Google is case-insensitive. If you search for Three, three, THREE, even ThrEE, you get the same results.

Full-Word Wildcards

Some search engines support a technique called *stemming*. Stemming is adding a wildcard character—usually * (asterisk) but sometimes ? (question mark)—to part of your query, requesting the search engine return variants of that query using the wildcard as a placeholder for the rest of the word at hand. For example, `moon*` would find: moons, moonlight, moonshot, etc.

Google doesn't support stemming.

Instead, Google offers the full-word wildcard. While you can't have a wildcard stand in for part of a word, you can insert a wildcard (Google's wildcard character is *) into a phrase and have the wildcard act as a substitute for one full word. Searching for `"three * mice"`, therefore, finds: three blind mice, three blue mice, three green mice, etc.

What good is the full-word wildcard? It's certainly not as useful as stemming, but then again, it's not as confusing to the beginner. One * is a stand-in for one word; two * signifies two words, and so on. The full-word wildcard comes in handy in the following situations:

- Avoiding the 10-word limit (see "The 10-Word Limit" next) on Google queries. You'll most frequently run into these examples when you're trying to find song lyrics or a quote. Plugging the phrase "Fourscore and seven years ago, our fathers brought forth on this continent" into Google will search only as far as the word "on"; everything thereafter is summarily ignored by Google.

- Checking the frequency of certain phrases and derivatives of phrases, like: `intitle:"methinks the * doth protest too much"` and `intitle: "the * of Seville"` (`intitle:` is described later in "Special Syntax").

- Filling in the blanks on a fitful memory. Perhaps you remember only a short string of song lyrics; search using only what you remember rather than randomly reconstructed full lines.

Let's take as an example the disco anthem "Good Times" by Chic. Consider the line: "You silly fool, you can't change your fate."

Perhaps you've heard that lyric, but you can't remember if the word "fool" is correct or if it's something else. If you're wrong (if the correct line is, for example, "You silly child, you can't change your fate"), your search will find no results and you'll come away with the sad conclusion that no one on the Internet has bothered to post lyrics to Chic songs.

The solution is to run the query with a wildcard in place of the unknown word, like so:

```
"You silly *, you can't change your fate"
```

You can use this technique for quotes, song lyrics, poetry, and more. You should be mindful, however, to include enough of the quote that you find unique results. Searching for "you * fool" will glean you far too many irrelevant hits.

The 10-Word Limit

Unless you're fond of long, detailed queries, you might never have noticed that Google has a hard limit of 10 words—that's keywords and special syntaxes combined—ignoring anything beyond. While this has no real effect on casual Google users, search hounds quickly find this limit rather cramps their style.

Favor Obscurity

By limiting your query to the more obscure of your keywords or phrase fragments, you'll hone results without squandering precious query words. Let's say you're

---

interested in a phrase from Hamlet: "The lady doth protest too much, methinks." At first blush, you might simply paste the entire phrase into the query field. But that's 7 of your 10 allotted words right there, leaving no room for additional query words or search syntax.

The first thing to do is ditch the first couple of words; "The lady" is just too common a phrase. This leaves the 5 words "doth protest too much, methinks." Neither "methinks" nor "doth" are words you might hear every day, providing a nice Shakespearean anchor for the phrase. That said, one or the other should suffice, leaving the query at an even 4 words with room to grow:

```
"protest too much methinks"
```

or:

```
"doth protest too much"
```

Either of these will provide you, within the first five results, origins of the phrase and pointers to more information.

Unfortunately, this technique won't do you much good in the case of "Do as I say, not as I do," which doesn't provide much in the way of obscurity. Attempt clarification by adding something like quote origin English usage and you're stepping beyond the 10-word limit. One solution is described next.

Playing the Wildcard

Help comes in the form of Google's full-word wildcard, described earlier. It turns out that Google doesn't count wildcards toward the limit.

So, when you have more than 10 words, substitute a wildcard for common words, like so:

```
"do as * say not as * do" quote origin English usage
```

Presto! Google runs the search without complaint, and you're in for some well-honed results.

Special Syntax

In addition to the basic AND, OR, and phrase searches, Google offers some rather extensive special syntax for honing your searches.

As a full-text search engine, Google indexes entire web pages instead of just titles and descriptions. Additional commands, called *special syntax* or *advanced operators*, let Google users search specific parts of web pages for specific types of information. This comes in handy when you're dealing with more than 3 billion web pages and need every opportunity to narrow your search results. Specifying that your query words must appear only in the title or URL of a returned web page is a great way to have your results get very specific without making your keywords themselves too specific. Following are descriptions of the special syntax elements, ordered by common usage and function.

NOTE

Some of these syntax elements work well in combination. Others fare not quite as well. Still others do not work at all. For detailed discussion on what does and does not mix, see "Mixing Syntax."

---

intitle:

intitle: restricts your search to the titles of web pages. The variation allintitle: finds pages wherein all the words specified appear in the title of the web page. Using allintitle: is basically the same as using the intitle: before each keyword.

    intitle:"george bush"
    allintitle:"money supply" economics

You may wish to avoid the allintitle: variation, because it doesn't mix well with some of the other syntax elements.

intext:

`intext:` searches only body text (i.e., ignores link text, URLs, and titles). While its uses are limited, it's perfect for finding query words that might be too common in URLs or link titles.

```
intext:"yahoo.com"
intext:html
```

There's an `allintext:` variation, but again, this doesn't play well with others.

inanchor:

`inanchor:` searches for text in a page's link anchors. A link anchor is the descriptive text of a link. For example, the link anchor in the HTML code `<a href="http://www.oreilly.com">O'Reilly and Associates</a>` is "O'Reilly and Associates."

```
inanchor:"tom peters"
```

As with other `in*:` syntax elements, there's an `allinanchor:` variation, which works in a similar way (i.e., all the keywords specified must appear in a page's link anchors).

site:

`site:` allows you to narrow your search by either a site or a top-level domain. The AltaVista search engine, by contrast, has two syntax elements for this function (`host:` and `domain:`), but Google has only the one.

```
site:loc.gov
site:thomas.loc.gov
site:edu
site:nc.us
```

Be aware that `site:` is no good for trying to search for a page that exists beneath the main or default site (i.e., in a subdirectory like */~sam/album/*). For example, if you're looking for something below the main GeoCities site, you can't use `site:` to find all the pages in *http://www.geocities.com/Heartland/Meadows/6485/*; Google returns no results. Use `inurl:` instead.

inurl:

inurl: restricts your search to the URLs of web pages. This syntax tends to work well for finding search and help pages, because they tend to be rather regular in composition. An allinurl: variation finds all the words listed in a URL but doesn't mix well with some other special syntax.

```
inurl:help
allinurl:search help
```

You'll see that using the inurl: query instead of the site: query has two immediate advantages:

- You can use inurl: by itself without using any other query words, something you can't do with site:.
- You can use it to search subdirectories.

NOTE

While the http:// prefix in a URL is ignored by Google when used with site:, search results come up short when including it in an inurl: query. Be sure to remove prefixes in any inurl: query for the best (read: any) results.

You can also use inurl: in combination with the site: syntax to get information about subdomains. For example, how many subdomains does *oreilly.com* really have? You can't get that information via the query site:oreilly.com, nor can you get it just from the query inurl:"*.oreilly.com" (because that query will pick up mirrors and other URLs containing the string *oreilly.com* that aren't at the O'Reilly site).

However, this query will work just fine:

```
site:oreilly.com inurl:"*.oreilly" -inurl:"www.oreilly"
```

This query asks Google to search the *oreilly.com* domain for subdomains with page URLs that contain the string *.oreilly* but ignore URLs with the string *www.oreilly* (since you're already quite familiar with that particular subdomain).

link:

link: returns a list of pages linking to the specified URL. Enter link: www.google.com and you'll get a list of pages that link to Google. Don't worry about including the http:// bit; you don't need it and, indeed, Google appears to ignore it even if you do put it in. link: works just as well with "deep" URLs—*http://www. raelity.org/apps/blosxom/*, for instance—as with top-level URLs such as *raelity.org*.

cache:

cache: finds a copy of the page that Google indexed even if that page is no longer available at its original URL or has since changed its content completely.

    `cache:www.yahoo.com`

If Google returns a result that appears to have little to do with your query, you're almost sure to find what you're looking for in the latest cached version of the page at Google.

The Google cache is particularly useful for retrieving a previous version of a page that changes often.

daterange:

daterange: limits your search to a particular date or range of dates that a page was indexed. It's important to note that a daterange: search has nothing to do with when a page was created, but when it was indexed by Google. So a page created on February 2 and not indexed by Google until April 11 would turn up in a daterange: search for April 11.

Remember also that Google reindexes pages. Whether the date range changes depends on whether the page content has changed. For example, Google indexes a page on June 1 and reindexes the page on August 13, but the page content hasn't changed. The date for the purposes of a daterange: search is still June 1.

While the daterange:syntax functions as you would expect, Google doesn't stand behind the results of a date-range search. So if you get a weird result, you can't complain to them. Google would rather you use the date-range options on their Advanced Search page (see "Advanced Search"); unfortunately, the Advanced Search allows you to restrict your options only to the last three months, six months, or year.

Why would you want to search by daterange:? There are several reasons:

- It narrows your search results to fresher content. Google might find some obscure, out-of-the-way page and index it only once. Two years later, this never-updated page is still turning up in your search results. Limiting your search to a more recent date range will result in only the most current of matches.

- It helps you dodge current events. Say John Doe sets a world record for eating hot dogs and immediately afterward rescues a baby from a burning building. Less than a week after that happens, Google's search results are going to be filled with John Doe. If you're searching for information on another John Doe, babies, or burning buildings, you'll scarcely be able to get rid of him.

  However, you can avoid Mr. Doe's exploits by setting the date-range syntax to before the hot dog contest. This also works well for avoiding recent, heavily covered news events, such as a crime spree or a forest fire, and annual events of at least national importance, such as national elections or the Olympics.

- It allows you to compare results over time; for example, if you want to search for occurrences of "Mac OS X" and "Windows XP" over time.

  Of course, a count like this isn't foolproof; indexing dates change over time. But generally it works well enough that you can spot trends.

Using the daterange: syntax is as simple as:

daterange:*startdate-enddate*

The catch is that the date must be expressed as a Julian date, a continuous count of days since noon UTC (Coordinated Universal Time) on January 1, 4713 B.C. So, for example, July 8, 2002 is Julian date 2452463.5, and May 22, 1968 is 2439998.5. Furthermore, Google isn't fond of decimals in its daterange:

queries; use only integers: 2452463 or 2452464 (depending on whether you prefer to round up or down) in the previous example. For more information on Julian dates, see the Appendix (Part V).

NOTE

The daterange: syntax demands that you always specify a start date and an end date. If you're looking for one day in particular, use the same Julian date for both *startdate* and *enddate*.

You can use the daterange: syntax with most other Google special syntax elements, with the exception of the link: syntax, which doesn't mix well with other special syntax, and Google's Special Collections (e.g., stocks: and phonebook:), described in Part IV.

daterange: does wonders for narrowing your search results. Let's look at a couple of examples.

Geri Halliwell left the Spice Girls around May 27, 1998. If you wanted to get a lot of information about the breakup, you could try doing a date search in a 10-day window—say, May 25 to June 4. That query would look like this:

```
"Geri Halliwell" "Spice Girls" daterange:2450958-2450968
```

At the time of this writing, you'll get about two dozen results, including several news stories about the breakup. If you wanted to find less formal sources, Geri or "Ginger Spice", instead of "Geri Halliwell", would work nicely.

That example's a bit on the silly side, but you get the idea. Any event with clearly delineated before and after dates—an event, a death, an overwhelming change in circumstances—can be reflected in a date-range search.

You can also use an individual event's date to change the results of a larger search. For example, former ImClone CEO Sam Waksal was arrested on June 12, 2002. You don't have to search for the name Sam Waskal to get a very narrow set of results for June 13, 2002:

```
imclone daterange:2452439-2452439
```

Similarly, if you search for imclone before the date of 2452439, you'll get very different results. As an interesting exercise, try a search that reflects the arrest, but date it a few days before the actual arrest:

```
imclone investigated daterange:2452000-2452435
```

This is a good way to find information or analysis that predates the actual event, but that provides background that might help explain the event itself. (Unless you use the date-range search, usually this kind of information is buried underneath news of the event itself.)

But what about narrowing your search results based on content creation date?

Searching by Content Creation Date

Searching for materials based on content creation is difficult. There's no standard date format (score one for Julian dates), many people don't date their pages anyway, some pages don't contain date information in their header, and still other content management systems routinely stamp pages with today's date, confusing things still further.

We can offer a few suggestions for searching by content creation date. Try adding a string of common date formats to your query. If you wanted something from May 2003, for example, you could try appending:

```
("May * 2003" | "May 2003" | 05/03 | 05/*/03)
```

(Remember that the | represents OR.) A query like that uses up most of your 10-word limit, however, so it's best to be judicious—perhaps by cycling through these formats one at a time. If any one of these is giving you too many results, try restricting your search to the title tag of the page, using intitle:.

If you're feeling really lucky, you can search for a full date, like May 9, 2003. Your decision then is whether you want to search for the date in the previous format or as one of many variations: 9 May 2003, 9/5/2003, 9 May 03, and so forth. Exact-date searching will severely limit your results and should be used only as a last-ditch effort.

When using date-range searching, you'll have to be flexible in your thinking, more general in your search than you otherwise would be (because the date-range search will narrow your results substantially), and persistent in your queries, because different dates and date ranges will yield very different results. That said, you'll be rewarded with smaller result sets focused on very specific events and topics in time.

filetype:

`filetype:` searches the suffixes or filename extensions. These are usually, but not necessarily, different file types; `filetype:htm` and `filetype:html` will give you different result counts, even though they're the same file type. You can even search for different page generators—such as ASP, PHP, CGI, and so forth—presuming the site isn't hiding them behind redirection and proxying. Google indexes several different Microsoft formats, including: Power-Point (*.ppt*), Excel (*.xls*), and Word (*.doc*).

```
homeschooling filetype:pdf
"leading economic indicators" filetype:ppt
```

related:

`related:`, as you might expect, finds pages that are related to the specified page. This is a good way to find categories of pages; a search for `related:google.com` returns a variety of search engines, including HotBot, Yahoo!, and Northern Light.

```
related:www.yahoo.com
related:www.cnn.com
```

While an increasingly rare occurrence, you'll find that not all pages are related to other pages.

info:

`info:` provides a page of links to more information about a specified URL. This information includes a link to the URL's cache, a list of pages that link to the URL, pages that are related to the URL, and pages that contain the URL.

```
info:www.oreilly.com
info:www.nytimes.com/technology
```

Note that this information is dependent on whether Google has indexed the specified URL; if not, information will obviously be far more limited.

phonebook:

phonebook:, as you might expect, looks up phone numbers.

```
phonebook:John Doe CA
phonebook:(510) 555-1212
```

The phonebook is covered in detail in "Consulting the Phonebook" in Part IV.

Mixing Syntax

There was a time when you couldn't mix Google's special syntax elements—you were limited to one per query. And while Google released ever more powerful special syntax elements, not being able to combine them for their composite power stunted many a search.

This has since changed. While there remain some syntax elements that you just can't mix, there are plenty to combine in clever and powerful ways. A thoughtful combination can do wonders to narrow a search.

How Not to Mix Syntax

There are some simple rules to follow when mixing syntax elements. These, for the most part, revolve around how *not* to mix:

- Don't mix syntax elements that will cancel each other out, such as:

  ```
  site:ucla.edu -inurl:ucla
  ```

  Here you're saying you want all results to come from *ucla.edu*, but that site results should not have the string "ucla" in the results. Obviously, that's not going to produce many URLs.

- Don't overuse single syntax elements, as in:

```
site:com site:edu
```

While you might think you're asking for results from either *.com* or *.edu* sites, what you're actually saying is that site results should come from both simultaneously. Obviously, a single result can come from only one domain. Take the example `perl site:edu site:com`. This search will get you exactly zero results. Why? Because a result page cannot come from a *.edu* domain and a *.com* domain at the same time. If you want results from *.edu* and *.com* domains only, rephrase your search like this:

```
perl (site:edu | site:com)
```

With the pipe character (|), you're specifying that you want results to come either from the *.edu* or the *.com* domain.

- Don't use `allinurl:` or `allintitle:` when mixing syntax. It takes a careful hand not to misuse these in a mixed search. Instead, stick to `inurl:` or `intitle:`. If you don't put `allinurl:` in exactly the right place, you'll create odd search results. Let's look at this example:

```
allinurl:perl intitle:programming
```

At first glance, it looks like you're searching for the string "perl" in the result URL, and the word "programming" in the title. And you're right: this will work fine. But what happens if you move `allinurl:` to the right of the query?

```
intitle:programming allinurl:perl
```

This won't bring any results. Stick to `inurl:` and `intitle:`, which are much more forgiving of where you put them in a query.

The same advice goes for `allintext:` and `allinanchor:`.

- Don't use so much syntax that you get too narrow, like:

```
title:agriculture site:ucla.edu inurl:search
```

You might find that it's too narrow to give you any use-ful results. If you're trying to find something so specific that you think you'll need a narrow query, start by build-ing a little bit of the query at a time. Say you want to find plant databases at UCLA. Instead of starting with the query:

```
title:plants site:ucla.edu inurl:database
```

Try something simpler:

```
databases plants site:ucla.edu
```

and then try adding syntax to keywords you've already established in your search results:

```
intitle:plants databases site:ucla.edu
```

or:

```
intitle:database plants site:ucla.edu
```

How to Mix Syntax

If you're trying to narrow down search results, the `intitle:` and `site:` syntax elements are your best bet.

Titles and sites. For example, say you want to get an idea of what databases are offered by the state of Texas. Run this search:

```
intitle:search intitle:records site:tx.us
```

You'll find something on the order of 50 very targeted results. And, of course, you can narrow down your search even more by adding keywords:

```
birth intitle:search intitle:records site:tx.us
```

It doesn't seem to matter whether you put plain keywords at the beginning or the end of the search query; I put them at the beginning, because they're easier to keep up with.

The `site:` syntax, unlike site syntax on other search engines, allows you to get as general as a domain suffix (`site:com`) or as specific as a domain or subdomain (`site:thomas.loc.gov`).

So if you're looking for records in El Paso, you can use this query:

```
intitle:records site:el-paso.tx.us
```

and you'll get around 10 results.

Title and URL. Sometimes you'll want to find a certain type of information, but you don't want to narrow by type. Instead, you want to narrow by theme of information (e.g., you want help or a search engine). That's when you need to search in the URL.

The inurl: syntax will search for a string in the URL but won't count finding it within a larger word. So, for example, if you search for inurl: research, Google will not find pages from *researchbuzz.com*, but it will find pages from *www. research-councils.ac.uk*.

Say you want to find information on biology, with an emphasis on learning or assistance. Try:

```
intitle:biology inurl:help
```

This takes you to a manageable 150 or so results. The whole point is to get a number of results that finds you what you need but isn't so large as to be overwhelming. If you find 150 results overwhelming, you can easily mix the site: syntax into the search and limit your results to universities:

```
intitle:biology inurl:help site:edu
```

Beware, however, of using too much special syntax. As mentioned earlier, you can quickly detail yourself into no results at all.

The Antisocial Syntax Elements

The antisocial syntax elements are the ones that won't mix and should be used individually for maximum effect. If you try to use them with other syntax elements, you won't get any results.

The syntax elements that request special information—stocks:, rphonebook:, bphonebook:, and phonebook: (see Part IV for details)—are all antisocial. That is, you can't mix them and expect to get a reasonable result.

The other antisocial syntax is link:. The link: syntax shows you which pages have a link to a specified URL. Wouldn't it be great if you could specify what domains you wanted the pages to be from? Sorry, you can't. The link: domain does not mix with anything else—not even plain old keywords.

For example, say you want to find out what pages link to O'Reilly & Associates, Inc., but you don't want to include pages from the *.edu* domain. The query link:www.oreilly. com -site:edu will not work, because of the link: syntax's inability to work in combination. Well, that's not quite correct; you will get results, but they'll be for the phrase "link: www.oreilly.com" from domains that are not *.edu*.

If you want to search for links and exclude the *.edu* domain, there's no single command that will absolutely work. This one's a good try, though:

```
inanchor:oreilly -inurl:oreilly -site:edu
```

This search looks for the word "oreilly" in anchor text, the text that's used to define links. It excludes pages that contain "oreilly" in the search result (e.g., *oreilly.com*). And, finally, it excludes those pages that come from the *.edu* domain.

But this type of search is nowhere approaching complete. It only finds those links to O'Reilly that include the string "oreilly": if someone creates a link like <a href="http:// perl.oreilly.com/">Camel Book</a>, it won't be found by the preceding query. Furthermore, there are other domains that contain the string "oreilly", and there may be domains that link to "oreilly" that contain the string "oreilly" but aren't *oreilly.com*. You could alter the string slightly, to omit the *oreilly.com* site itself but not other sites containing the string "oreilly":

```
inanchor:oreilly -site:oreilly.com -site:edu
```

However, you would still be including many O'Reilly sites—
XML.com and *MacDevCenter.com*, for instance—that aren't at *oreilly.com*.

All the Possibilities

While it is possible to write down every syntax-mixing combination and briefly explain how they might be useful, there wouldn't be room for much else in this book.

Experiment. Experiment a lot. Keep in mind constantly that most of these syntax elements do not stand alone, and you can get more done by combining them than by using them one at a time.

Depending on what kind of research you are doing, different patterns will emerge over time. For example, you may discover that focusing on only PDF documents (`filetype:pdf`) finds you the results you need. You may discover that you should concentrate on specific file types in specific domains (`filetype:ppt site:tompeters.com`). Mix up the syntax in as many ways as is relevant to your research and see what you get.

As with anything else, the more you use Google's special syntax, the more natural it will become to you. And Google is constantly adding more, much to the delight of regular web-combers.

If, however, you want something more structured and visual than a single query line, Google's Advanced Search should fit the bill.

Advanced Search

Google's default simple search allows you to do quite a bit, but not everything. Google's Advanced Search page (*http://www.google.com/advanced_search?hl=en*), shown in Figure 7, provides more options such as date search and filtering, with "fill in the blank" searching options for those who don't take naturally to memorizing special syntax.

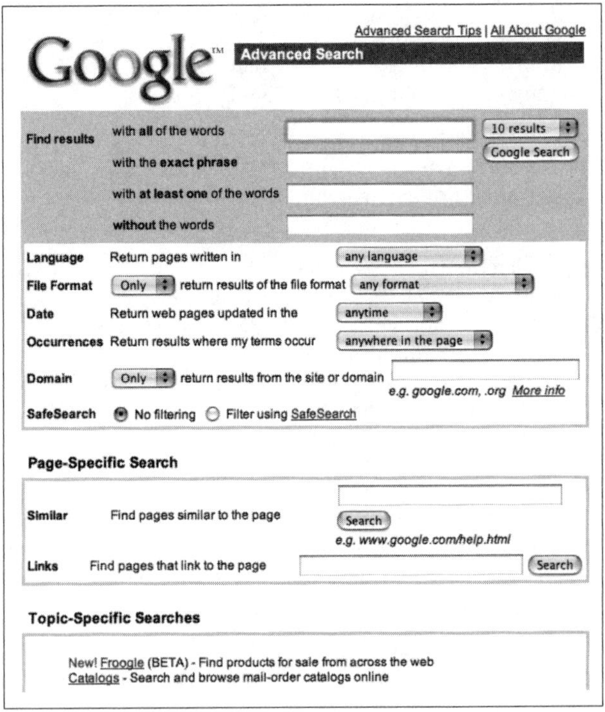

Figure 7. Google's Advanced Search page

Most of the options presented on this page are self-explanatory, but we'll take a quick look at the kinds of searches that you really can't do easily using the simple search's single-text-field interface.

Query Words

Because Google uses Boolean AND by default, it's sometimes hard to logically build out the nuances of just the query you're aiming for. Using the text boxes at the top of the Advanced Search page, you can specify words that *must* appear—exact phrases, lists of words, at least one of which must appear—and words to be excluded.

Language

Using the Language pull-down menu, you can specify what language all returned pages must be in, from Arabic to Turkish.

File Format

The File Format option lets you include or exclude several different file formats, including Microsoft Word and Excel. There are a couple of Adobe formats (most notably PDF) and Rich Text Format as options here too. This is where the Advanced Search is at its most limited; there are literally dozens of file formats that Google can search for, and this set of options represents only a small subset. To get at the others, use the filetype: special syntax described earlier in "Special Syntax."

Date

Date allows you to specify search results updated in the last three months, six months, or year. This date search is much more limited than the daterange: special syntax, which can give you results as narrow as one day, but Google stands behind the results generated using the Date option on the Advanced Search, while not officially sanctioning the use of the daterange: search.

Occurrences

Using the Occurrences pull-down menu, you can specify where the terms should occur. The options here, other than the default, generally reflect the allin*: syntax elements—in the title of the page (allintitle:), in the text of the page (allintext:), in the URL of the page (allinurl:), and in the page's link anchors (allinanchor:).

Domain

The Domain feature is an interface to the site: syntax. It also allows negation, explained earlier, to explicitly *not* return results from a site or domain.

Safe Search

Google's Advanced Search further gives you the option to filter your results using SafeSearch. SafeSearch filters only explicit sexual content (as opposed to some filtering systems that filter pornography, hate material, gambling information, etc.). Please remember that machine filtering isn't 100% perfect.

Additional Google Properties

The rest of the page provides individual search forms for other Google properties, including a news search, a page-specific search, and links to some of Google's topic-specific searches. The news search and other topic-specific searches work independently of the main Advanced Search form at the top of the page.

The Advanced Search page is handy when you need to use its unique features or you need some help putting a complicated query together. Its "fill in the blank" interface will come in handy for the occasional searcher or someone who wants to get an advanced search exactly right. That said, it is limiting in other ways; it's difficult to use mixed syntax or build a single syntax search using OR. For example, there's no way to search for site:edu OR site:org using the Advanced Search. This search must be done from the Google search box.

Of course, there's another way you can alter the search results that Google gives you, and it doesn't involve the basic search input or the Advanced Search page. It's the preferences page, described in "Setting Preferences" in Part III.

Specialized Vocabularies: Slang and Terminology

When a teenager says something is "phat," that's slang—a specialized vocabulary for a certain section of the world culture. When a copywriter scribbles "stet" on an ad, that's not slang, but it's still specialized vocabulary or jargon for a certain section of the world culture—in this case, the advertising industry.

We have distinctive speech patterns that are shaped by our educations, our families, and where we live. Further, we may use another set of words based on our occupation.

Being aware of these specialty words can make all the difference in the world when it comes to searching. Adding specialized words to your search query—whether slang or industry vocabulary—can really change the slant of your search results.

Slang

Slang gives you one more way to break up your search-engine results into geographically distinct areas. There's some geographical blurriness when you use slang to narrow your search-engine results, but it's amazing how well it works. For example, search Google for football. Now search for football bloke. Totally different results set, isn't it? Now

---

search for football bloke bonce. Now you're into soccer narratives.

Of course, this is not to say that everyone in England automatically uses the word "bloke" any more than everyone in the southern U.S. automatically uses the word "y'all." But adding well-chosen bits of slang (which will take some experimentation) will give a whole different tenor to your search results and may point you in unexpected directions. You can find slang from the following resources:

The Probert Encyclopedia—Slang
This site is browseable by first letter or searchable by keyword. (Note that the keyword search covers the entire *Probert Encyclopedia*—slang results are near the bottom.) Slang is from all over the world. It's often cross-linked, especially drug slang. As with most slang dictionaries, this site contains materials that might offend.

> *http://www.probertencyclopaedia.com/slang.htm*

A Dictionary of Slang
This site focuses on slang heard in the United Kingdom, which means slang from other places as well. It's browseable by letter or via a search engine. Words from outside the U.K. are marked with their place of origin in brackets. Definitions also indicate typical usage: humorous, vulgar, derogatory, etc.

> *http://www.peevish.co.uk/slang/*

Surfing for Slang
Of course, each area in the world has its own slang. This site has a good meta-list of English and Scandinavian slang resources.

> *http://www.linkopp.com/members/vlaiko/slanglinks.htm*

Start out by searching Google for your query without the slang. Check the results and decide where they're falling short. Are they not specific enough? Are they not located in

---

the right geographical area? Are they not covering the right demographic—teenagers, for example?

Introduce one slang word at a time. For example, for a search for "football," add the word "bonce" and check the results. If they're not narrowed down enough, add the word "bloke." Add one word at a time until you get to the kind of results you want. Using slang is an inexact science, so you'll have to do some experimenting.

Here are some things to be careful of when using slang in your searches:

- Try many different slang words.
- Don't use slang words that are generally considered offensive, except as a last resort. Your results will be skewed.
- Be careful when using teenage slang, which changes constantly.
- Try searching for slang when using Google Groups. Slang crops up often in conversation.
- Minimize your searches for slang when searching for more formal sources like newspaper stories.
- Don't use slang phrases if you can help it; in my experience, slang changes too much to be consistently searchable. Stick to words.

Specialized Vocabularies—Industrial Slang

Specialized vocabularies are those used in particular subject areas and industries. The medical and legal fields are good examples of specialized vocabularies, although there are many others.

When you need to tip your search to the more technical, the more specialized, and the more in-depth, think of a specialized vocabulary. For example, do a Google search for heartburn. Now do a search for heartburn GERD. Now do a search for heartburn GERD "gastric acid". You'll see each of them is very different.

With some fields, finding specialized-vocabulary resources will be a snap. But with others it's not that easy. As a jumping-off point, try the Glossarist site at *http://www.glossarist.com*; it's a searchable subject index of about 6,000 different glossaries covering dozens of different topics. There are also several other large, online resources covering certain specific vocabularies. These resources include:

The On-Line Medical Dictionary

This dictionary contains vocabulary relating to biochemistry, cell biology, chemistry, medicine, molecular biology, physics, plant biology, radiobiology, science, and technology, and currently has over 46,000 listings.

You can browse the dictionary by letter or search it by word. Sometimes you can search for a word that you know (bruise) and find another term that might be more common in medical terminology (contusion). You can also browse the dictionary by subject. Bear in mind that this dictionary is in the U.K. and some spellings may be slightly different for American users ("tumour" versus "tumor", etc.).

http://cancerweb.ncl.ac.uk/omd/

MedTerms.com

MedTerms.com has far fewer definitions (around 10,000), but it also has extensive articles from MedicineNet. If you're starting from absolute square one with your research and you need some basic information and vocabulary to get started, search MedicineNet for your term (bruise works well) and then move to MedTerms.com to search for specific words.

http://www.medterms.com/

Law.com's legal dictionary

Law.com's legal dictionary is excellent because you can search either words or definitions; you can browse, too. For example, you can search definitions for the word inheritance and get a list of all the entries that contain the word "inheritance". This is an easy way to get to the words "muniment of title" without knowing the path.

http://dictionary.law.com/lookup2.asp

As with slang, add specialized vocabulary slowly—one word at a time—and anticipate that it will narrow down your search results very quickly. For example, take the word "spudding," often used in association with oil drilling. Searching for spudding by itself finds only about 2,500 results on Google. Adding Texas knocks it down to 525 results, and this is still a very general search! Add specialized vocabulary very carefully or you'll narrow down your search results to the point where you can't find what you want.

PART III

Understanding What You Get

Whew! By now it should be fairly clear that a simple interface such as the one Google has on its front page does not necessarily imply limited power. Still waters run deep indeed. Now that we have all of the tools, tips, and techniques under our belt to help us ask Google for what we want before it dives into the depths of web content, it's time to turn our attention to understanding what it brings back to the surface.

In this part of the book, we'll look at getting Google to remember how you like to see results presented and how to interpret the list of results that are presented on the results page. We'll also take a brief foray into the world of Google URLs and how to tweak them to your advantage. Finally, we'll look at embracing Google's penchant for spelling.

Setting Preferences

Google's Preferences page, shown in Figure 8, provides a nice, easy way to set your searching preferences from this moment forward.

Interface Language

You can set your Interface Language, affecting the language in which tips and messages are displayed. Language choices range from Afrikaans to Zulu, with plenty of odd options, including Bork, bork, bork! (the Swedish Chef), Elmer Fudd, and Pig Latin thrown in for fun.

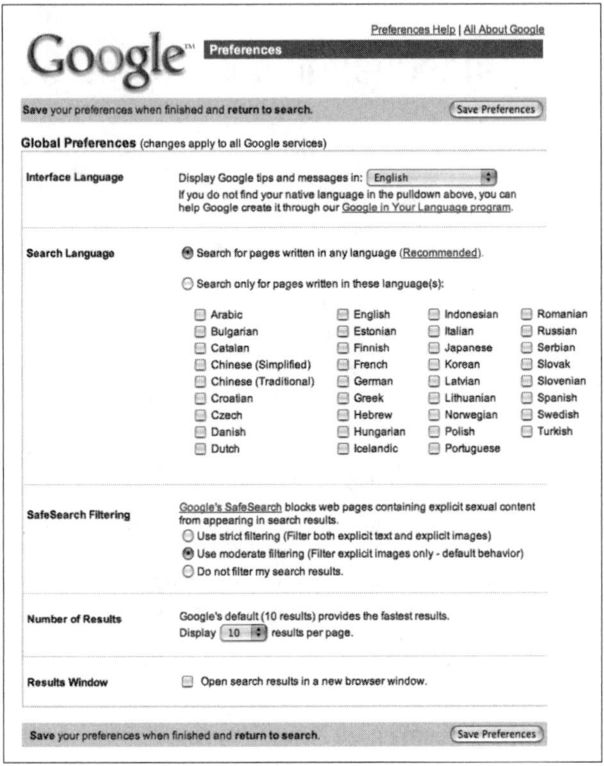

Figure 8. Google's Preferences page

Search Language

Not to be confused with Interface Language, Search Language restricts what languages should be considered when searching Google's page index. The default is any language, but you could be interested only in web pages written in Chinese and Japanese, or French, German, and Spanish—the combination is up to you.

SafeSearch Filtering

Google's SafeSearch filtering affords you a method of avoiding search results that may offend your sensibilities. No filtering means you're offered anything in the Google index. Moderate filtering rules out explicit images, but not explicit language. Strict filtering filters both text and images. The default is moderate filtering.

Number of Results

By default, Google displays 10 results per page. For more results, click any of the "Result Page: 1 2 3..." links at the bottom of each result page, or simply click the "Next" link.

You can specify your preferred number of results per page (10, 20, 30, 50, or 100), along with whether you want results to open in the current window or a new browser window.

Settings for Researchers

For the purpose of research, it's best to have as many search results as possible on the page. Because it's all text, it doesn't take that much longer to load 100 results than it does to load 10. If you have a computer with a decent amount of memory, it's also good to have search results open in a new window; it'll keep you from losing your place and leave you a window with all the search results constantly available.

If you can stand it, leave your filtering turned off, or at least limit the filtering to moderate instead of strict. Machine filtering is not perfect and, unfortunately, having filtering on sometimes means you might miss something valuable. This is especially true when you're searching for words that might be caught by a filter, like "breast cancer."

Unless you're absolutely sure that you always want to do a search in one language, I'd advise against setting your language preferences on this page. Instead, alter language preferences as needed using the Google Language Tools (see Part IV).

Between the simple search, advanced search, and preferences, you've got all the tools necessary to build the Google query to suit your particular purposes.

WARNING

If you have cookies turned off in your browser, setting preferences in Google isn't going to do you much good. You'll have to reset them every time you open your browser. If you can't have cookies and you want to use the same preferences every time, consider making a customized search form.

Anatomy of a Search Result

You'd think a list of search results would be pretty straightforward, wouldn't you—just a page title and a link, possibly a summary? Not so with Google. Google encompasses so many search properties and has so much data at its disposal that it fills every results page to the rafters. Within a typical search result you can find sponsored links, ads, links to stock quotes, page sizes, spelling suggestions, and more.

By knowing more of the nitty-gritty details of what's what in a search result, you'll be able to make some guesses ("Wow, this page that links to my page is very large; perhaps it's a link list") and correct roadblocks ("I can't find my search term on this page; I'll check the version Google has cached").

Let's use the word "flowers" to examine this anatomy. Figure 9 shows the result page for flowers.

First, you'll note at the top of the page is a selection of tabs, allowing you to repeat your search across other Google search categories besides web pages, including Google Groups, Google Images, and the Google Directory (all described in Part IV). Beneath that you'll see a count for the number of results and how long the search took: about 13,700,000 results in 0.11 seconds, as shown in Figure 10.

Figure 9. Result page for "flowers"

Figure 10. Google search-property tabs and results count

Sometimes you'll see results/sites called out on colored backgrounds at the top or right of the results page (see Figure 11). These are called *sponsored links* (read: advertisements). Google has a policy of very clearly distinguishing ads and sticking to text-based advertising only rather than throwing flashing banners in your face like many other sites do.

Beneath the sponsored links you sometimes see a category list. The category for flowers, as seen in Figure 12, is Shopping > Flowers > Wire Services. You'll see a category list only if you're searching for very general terms and your search consists of only one word. For example, if you searched for pinwheel flowers, Google wouldn't present the flowers category.

Figure 11. Sponsored links

Figure 12. Google Directory category listing

Why are you seeing category results? After all, Google is a full-text search engine, isn't it? It's because Google has taken the information from the Open Directory Project (*http://www.dmoz.org*) and crossed it with its own popularity rankings to make the Google Directory. When you see categories, you're seeing information from the Google Directory.

The first real (i.e., nonsponsored) result of the search for flowers is shown in Figure 13.

> 1-800-**FLOWERS**.COM - **Flowers**, Plants, Gourmet and
> Sweets, Unique ...
> **Flowers**, unique gifts, gourmet foods, sweets, plants and Specialty
> Boutique items
> presented by 1-800-**FLOWERS**.COM, a leading online provider of
> fresh-cut **flowers** ...
> www.800flowers.com/flowers/welcome.asp?section=0 - 36k -
> Cached - Similar pages

Figure 13. A typical search result

Let's break that down into chunks.

The top line of each result is the page title, hyperlinked to the original page.

The second line offers a brief extract from this site. Sometimes this is a description or a sentence or so. Sometimes it's HTML mush. Google tends to use description metatags when they're available; it's rare that you can't look at a Google search result for even a modicum of an idea what the site is all about.

The next line sports several informative bits of metadata. First, there's the URL; second, the size of the page (Google will have the page size available only if the page has been cached). There's a link to a cached version of the page if one is available. Finally, there's a link to find similar pages.

Why would you bother reading the search-result metadata? Why not simply visit the site and see if it has what you want?

If you've got a broadband connection and all the time in the world, you might not want to bother with checking out the metadata. But if you have a slower connection and time is at a premium, consider the search-result information.

First, check the page summary. Where does your keyword appear? Does it appear in the middle of a list of site names? Does it appear in a way that makes it clear that the context is not what you're looking for?

Check the size of the page if it's available. Is the page very large? Perhaps it's just a link list—a page full of hyperlinks, as the name suggests. Is it just 1 or 2K? It might be too small to find the detailed information you're looking for. If your aim is link lists, keep a lookout for pages larger than 20K and see "Finding Directories of Information" in Part IV.

Understanding Google URLs

If you're like most people, you usually pay little attention to the URLs in your browser's address bar as you surf from one site to the next. And you might choose to stick to this policy while searching Google. You ought to know, however, that a subtle alteration made to the URL that Google returns after a

(the "months old" modifier) it's the only way to get at a particular set of results.

Checking Spelling

If you've ever used other Internet search engines, you'll have experienced simplistic spellchecking. That's when you enter a proper noun and the search engine suggests a completely ludicrous query (e.g., "Elvish Parsley" for "Elvis Presley"). Google's quite a bit smarter than that.

When Google thinks it can spell individual words or complete phrases in your search query better than you can, it'll offer you a suggested "better" search, hyperlinking it directly to a query. For example, if you search for hydrocephelus, Google suggests that you search instead for hydrocephalus, as shown in Figure 14.

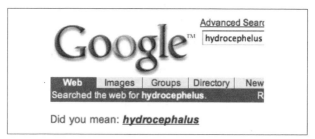

Figure 14. A Google spelling suggestion

Suggestions aside, Google will assume you know of what you speak and return your requested results—provided, that is, that your query gleaned results.

If your query found no results for the spellings you provided and Google believes it knows better, it will automatically run a new search on its own suggestions. Thus, a search for hydracefallus finding (hopefully) no results will spark a Google-initiated search for hydrocephalus.

Mind you, Google does not arbitrarily come up with its suggestions, but builds them based on its own database of words and phrases found while indexing the Web. If you search for nonsense like garafghafdghasdg, you'll get no results and be offered no suggestions, as Figure 15 shows.

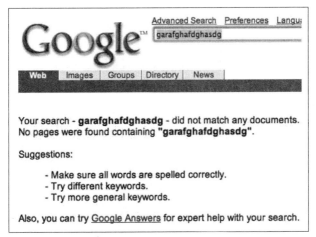

Figure 15. A search that yields no results

NOTE

Google's penchant for spellchecking has a lovely side effect: a quick-and-easy way to check the relative frequency of spellings. Query for a particular spelling, making note of the number of results. Then click on Google's suggested spelling and note the number of results. It's surprising how close the counts are sometimes, indicating an oft-misspelled word or phrase.

Embrace Misspellings

Don't make the mistake of automatically dismissing the proffered results from a misspelled word, particularly a proper name. I've been a fan of cartoonist Bill Mauldin for years now, but I continually misspell his name as "Bill Maudlin." And judging from a quick Google search, I'm not the only one. There is no law saying that every page must be spellchecked before it goes online, so it's often worth taking a look at results despite misspellings.

As an experiment, try searching for two misspelled words on a related topic, like `ventriculostemy hydrocephalis`. What kind of information did you get? Could the information you got, if any, be grouped into a particular online "genre"?

At the time of this writing, the search for `ventriculostemy hydrocephalis` gets only two results. Both of them are for a guestbook at the Developmental (Pediatric) Neurosurgery Unit at Massachusetts General Hospital/Harvard University. The content here is generally from people dealing with various neurosurgical problems. Again, there is no law that says all web materials, especially informal ones like guestbook communications, have to be spellchecked.

Use this to your advantage as a researcher. When you're looking for layman accounts of illness and injury, the content you desire might actually be misspelled more often than not. On the other hand, when looking for highly technical information or references from credible sources, filtering out misspelled queries will bring you closer to the information you seek.

PART IV

Other Google Services and Features

Now that you understand how to ask Google for what you want and how to understand what it gives you in return, that's pretty much it, right?

Not at all! Google is everyone's favorite web search engine, but it goes far beyond that. For the last couple of years, Google has been quietly adding properties and services that work in conjunction with the underlying search engine to give you a wide range of facilities, from mail-order catalogs to images, news, and newsgroups.

In addition to these special Google services, clever use of some of the all-but-undocumented components and features of the Google Web search engine will allow you to create your own virtual collections, check your spelling, track stocks, and more.

Google Directory

Google's Web search indexes over 3 billion pages, which means that it isn't suitable for all searches. When you've got a search that you can't narrow down—for example, if you're looking for information on a person about whom you know nothing—3 billion pages will get very frustrating very quickly.

But you don't have to limit your searches to the Web search. Google also has a searchable subject index, the Google Directory, at *http://directory.google.com*. Instead of indexing the entirety of billions of pages, the directory describes whole sites instead, indexing about 1.5 million URLs. This makes it a much better search for general topics, just a few of which are shown in Figure 16.

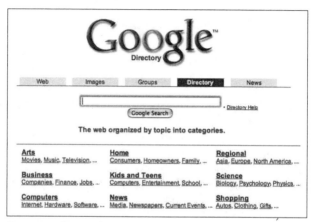

Figure 16. The Google Directory

Does Google spend time building a searchable subject index in addition to a full-text index? No. Google bases its directory on the Open Directory Project data at *http://dmoz.org*. The collection of URLs at the Open Directory Project is gathered and maintained by a group of volunteers, but Google does add some of its own Googlish magic to it.

As you can see, the front of the site is organized into several topics. To find what you're looking for, you can either do a keyword search, or "drill down" through the hierarchies of subjects.

Beside most of the listings, you'll see a green bar. The green bar is an approximate indicator of the site's PageRank™ (in the Google search engine. (Not every listing in the Google Directory has a corresponding PageRank in the Google web index.) Web sites are listed in the default order of Google

PageRank, but you also have the option to list them in alphabetical order.

NOTE

PageRank is Google's assessment of just how popular a page is. The higher the PageRank, the higher it'll appear in Google search results. See *http://www.google.com/ technology/index.html* and *Google Hacks*, Hack #95, "Inside the PageRank Algorithm" for more details.

One thing you'll notice about the Google Directory is how the annotations and other information varies between the categories. That's because the information in the directory is maintained by a small army of volunteers (about 20,000 at the time of this writing) who are each responsible for one or more categories. For the most part, annotation is pretty good.

Searching the Google Directory

The Google Directory does not have the various complicated special syntax elements for searching that the Web search does. That's because this is a far smaller collection of URLs, ideal for more general searching. However, there are a couple of special syntax elements you should know about:

intitle:
> Just like the Google web special syntax, intitle: restricts the query-word search to the title of a page.

inurl:
> Restricts the query-word search to the URL of a page.

When searching Google's web index, your overwhelming concern is probably how to get your list of search results to something manageable. With that in mind, you might start by coming up with the narrowest search possible. While that's certainly a reasonable strategy for the web index, because you have a narrower pool of sites in the Google Directory, you want to start more generally with your Google Directory search.

For example, say you were looking for information on author P. G. Wodehouse. A simple search on P. G. Wodehouse in Google's web index will get you over 56,000 results, possibly compelling you to immediately narrow down your search. But doing the same search in the Google Directory returns only 125 results. You might consider that a manageable number of results, or you might want to carefully start narrowing down your results further.

The Google Directory is also good for searching for events. A Google Web search for "Korean War" will find you literally hundreds of thousands of results, while searching the Google Directory will find you just over 1,200. This is a case where you will probably need to narrow down your search. Use general words indicating what kind of information you want—timeline, for example, or archives, or lesson plans. Don't narrow down your search with names or locations; that's not the best way to use the Google Directory.

Google Directory Special Syntax

Google Directory does not have any special search syntax.

Google Groups

Usenet Groups, text-based discussion groups covering literally hundreds of thousands of topics, have been around since long before the World Wide Web. They're available for search and perusal as Google Groups (*http://groups.google.com*). Its interface, shown in Figure 17, is rather different from the Google Web search, as all messages are divided into groups, and the groups themselves are divided into topics called *hierarchies*.

The Google Groups archive begins in 1981 and covers up to the present day. Over 200 million messages are archived. As you might imagine, that's a pretty big archive, covering literally decades of discussion. Stuck in an ancient computer game? Need help with that sewing machine you bought in 1982? You might be able to find the answers here.

Figure 17. Google Groups

Google Groups also allows you to participate in Usenet discussions, which is handy because not all ISPs provide access to Usenet these days (even those that tend to limit the number of newsgroups they carry). See the Google Groups posting FAQ (*http://groups.google.com/googlegroups/posting_faq.html*) for instructions on how to post to a newsgroup. You'll have to start with locating the group to which you want to post, and that means using the hierarchy.

There are regional and smaller hierarchies, but the main ones are *alt*, *biz*, *comp*, *humanities*, *misc*, *news*, *rec*, *sci*, *soc*, and *talk*. Most groups are created through a voting process and are put under the hierarchy that's most applicable to the topic.

Browsing Groups

From the main Google Groups page, you can browse through the list of groups by picking a hierarchy from the front page. You'll see there are subtopics, sub-subtopics, sub-sub-subtopics, and—well, you get the picture. For example, in the *comp* (computers) hierarchy, you'll find the subtopic *comp.sys*, or computer systems. Beneath that lie 75 groups and subtopics, including *comp.sys.mac*, a branch of the hierarchy devoted to the Macintosh computer system. There are 24 Mac subtopics, one of which is *comp.sys.mac. hardware*, which has, in turn, 3 groups beneath it. Once you've drilled down to the most specific group applicable to your interests, Google Groups presents the postings themselves, sorted in reverse chronological order.

This strategy works fine when you want to read a slow (very little traffic) or moderated group, but when you want to read a busy, free-for-all group, you may wish to use the Google Groups search engine. The search on the main page works very much like the regular Google search; your only clues that things are different is the Google Groups tab and each result has an associated group and posting date.

The Advanced Groups Search (*http://groups.google.com/ advanced_group_search*), however, looks much different. You can restrict your searches to a certain newsgroup or newsgroup topic. For example, you can restrict your search as broadly as the entire *comp* hierarchy (comp* would do it) or as narrowly as a single group like *comp.robotics.misc*. You can restrict messages to subject and author or by message ID.

NOTE

Of course, any options on the Advanced Groups Search page can be expressed via a little URL hacking (see "Understanding Google URLs" in Part III).

Possibly the biggest difference between Google Groups and Google Web search is the date searching. With Google Web search, date searching is notoriously inexact, referring to when a page was added to the index rather than the date the page was created. Each Google Groups message is stamped with the day it was actually posted to the newsgroup. Thus, the date searches on Google Groups are accurate and indicative of when content was produced. And, thankfully, they use the more familiar Gregorian dates rather than the Google Web search's Julian dates.

Google Groups Special Syntax

You can do some precise searching from the Google Advanced Groups Search page. And, just as with Google web, you have some special syntax at your disposal.

NOTE

Google Groups is an archive of conversations. Thus, when you're searching, you'll be more successful if you try looking for conversational and informal language, not the carefully structured language you'll find on Internet sites—well, some Internet sites, anyway.

---

intitle:

intitle: searches posting titles for query words.

```
intitle:rocketry
```

group:

group: restricts your search to a certain group or topic (set of groups). The wildcard * (asterisk) modifies a group: syntax to include everything beneath the specified group or topic. rec. humor* or rec.humor.* (effectively the same) will find results in the group *rec.humor*, as well as *rec.humor.funny*, *rec.humor.jewish*, and so forth.

```
group:rec.humor*
group:alt*
group:comp.lang.perl.misc
```

author:

author: specifies the author of a newsgroup post. This can be a full or partial name, even an email address.

```
author:fred
author:fred flintstone
author:flintstone@bedrock.gov
```

Mixing syntax in Google Groups. Google Groups is much more friendly to syntax mixing (see "Mixing Syntax" in Part II) than the Google Web search is. You can mix any syntax together in a Google Groups search, as exemplified by the following typical searches:

```
intitle:literature group:humanities* author:john
intitle:hardware group:comp.sys.ibm* pda
```

Some common search scenarios. There are several ways you can "mine" Google Groups for research information. Remember, though, to view any information you get here with a certain amount of skepticism—all Usenet is is hundreds of thousands of people tossing around links; in that respect, it's just like the Web.

Tech support. Ever used Windows and discovered that there's some program running you've never heard of? Uncomfortable, isn't it? If you're wondering if HIDSERV is something nefarious, Google Groups can tell you. Just search Google Groups for HIDSERV. You'll find that plenty of people had the same question before you did, and it's been answered.

I find that Google Groups is sometimes more useful than manufacturers' web sites. For example, I was trying to install a set of flight devices for a friend—a joystick, throttle, and rudder pedals. The web site for the manufacturer couldn't help me figure out why they weren't working. I described the problem as best I could in a Google Groups search—using the name of the parts and the manufacturer's brand name—and it wasn't easy, but I was able to find an answer.

Sometimes your problem isn't as serious but it's just as annoying; you might be stuck in a computer game. If the game has been out for more than a few months, your answer is probably in Google Groups. If you want the answer to an entire game, try the magic word "walkthrough." So if you're looking for a walkthrough for Quake II, try the search `"quake ii" walkthrough`. (You don't need to restrict your search to newsgroups; "walkthrough" is a word strongly associated with gamers.)

Finding commentary immediately after an event. With Google Groups, date searching is very precise (unlike date-searching Google's web index). So it's an excellent way to get commentary during or immediately after events.

Barbra Streisand and James Brolin were married on July 1, 1998. Searching for `"Barbra Streisand" "James Brolin"` between June 30, 1998 and July 3, 1998 leads to over 40 results, including reprinted wire articles, links to news stories, and commentary from fans. Searching for `"barbra streisand" "james brolin"` without a date specification finds more than 1,300 results.

Usenet is also much older than the Web and is ideal for finding information about an event that occured before the Web. Coca-Cola released "New Coke" in April 1985. You can find information about the release on the Web, of course, but finding contemporary commentary would be more difficult. After some playing around with the dates (just because it's been released doesn't mean it's in every store) I found plenty of commentary about "New Coke" in Google Groups by searching for the phrase `"new coke"` during the month of May 1985. Information included poll results, taste tests, and speculation on the new formula. Searching later in the summer yields information on Coke rereleasing old Coke under the name "Classic Coke."

Google Images

If you want to take a break from text crawling, check out Google Images (*http://images.google.com*), an index of over 425 million images available on the Web. While sorely lacking in special syntax, the Advanced Image Search (*http://images.google.com/advanced_ image_search*) does offer some interesting options.

Google Images starts with a plain keyword search. Images are indexed under a variety of keywords, some broader than others; be as specific as possible. If you're searching for cats, don't use cat as a keyword unless you don't mind getting results that include "CAT scan." Use words that are more uniquely cat-related, like feline or kitten. Narrow down your query as much as possible, using as few words as possible. A query like feline fang, which would get you over 3,000 results on Google, will get you no results on Google Image Search; in this case, cat fang works better. (Building queries for image searching takes a lot of patience and experimentation.)

Search results include a thumbnail, name, size (both pixels and kilobytes), and the URL where the picture is to be found. Figure 18 shows the results of a search for google hacks.

Clicking the picture will present a framed page with Google's thumbnail of the image at the top and the page where the image originally appeared at the bottom. Figure 19 shows a typical Google Images framed result page.

Searching Google Images can be a real gamble, because it's difficult to build multiple-word queries, and single-word queries lead to thousands of results. You do have more options to narrow your search both through the Advanced Image Search interface and through the Google Images special syntax.

Figure 18. Google Images search results

Figure 19. Google Images framed result page

The Google Advanced Image Search (*http://images.google. com/advanced_image_search*) allows you to specify the size (expressed in pixels, not kilobytes) of the returned image.

You can also specify the kind of pictures you want to find (Google Images indexes only JPEG, PNG, and GIF files), image color (black and white, grayscale, or full color), and any domain to which you wish to restrict your search.

Google Images also uses three levels of filtering: none, moderate, and strict. Moderate filters only explicit images, while strict filters both images and text. While automatic filtering doesn't guarantee that you won't find any offensive content, it will help. However, sometimes filtering works against you. If you're searching for images related to breast cancer, Google's strict filtering will greatly reduce your potential number of results. Any time you're using a word that might be considered offensive—even in an innocent context—you'll have to consider turning off the filters or risk missing relevant results. One way to get around the filterings is to try alternate words. If you're searching for breast-cancer images, try searching for mammograms or Tamoxifen, a drug used to treat breast cancer.

Google Images Special Syntax

Google Images offers a few special syntax elements.

intitle:

intitle: finds keywords in the page title. This is an excellent way to narrow down search results.

```
intitle:google
```

filetype:

filetype: finds pictures of a particular type. This works only for JPEG, PNG, and GIF, not BMP or any number of other formats Google doesn't index.

```
filetype:jpg
filetype:gif
```

Note that searching for filetype:jpg and filetype:jpeg will get you different results, even though they're both for JPEG images,

---

because the filtering is based on file extension, not some deeper understanding of the file type.

inurl:

`inurl:`, as with any regular Google search, finds the search term in the URL.

```
inurl:cat
inurl:dog.jpg
```

The results for this one can be confusing. For example, you may search for `inurl:cat` and get the following URL as part of the search result: *www.example.com/something/somethingelse/ something.html*

Hey, where's the cat? Because Google indexes the graphic name as part of the URL, it's probably there. If the page includes a graphic named *cat.jpg*, that's what Google is finding when you search for `inurl:cat`. It's finding the cat in the name of the picture, not in the URL itself.

site:

`site:`, as with any other Google Web search, restricts your results to a specified host or domain.

```
football site:uk
```

Don't use this to restrict results to a certain host unless you're really sure what's there. Instead, use it to restrict results to certain domains. For example, search for `football site:uk` and then search for `football`. The former turns up football (read: soccer) images, while the latter finds plenty for the American football fan.

`site:com` is a good example of how dramatic a difference using `site:` can make.

Google News

Google News (*http://news.google.com*) checks over 4,500 sources for news and current events, clustering headlines from disparate sources on its front page by story or subject matter. If you're a news hound, Google News is a good bet for up-to-the-minute updates on world and U.S. news, business, science and technology, sports, entertainment, and health. Figure 20 shows the Google News home page, updated just 7 minutes before this screenshot.

Figure 20. Google News

The search form functions like the Google Web search—all searches are default AND. Search results group similar news stories into clusters, providing title, source, date, and a brief summary (the link to the full story is included in the title). The only other option searchers have is to sort their searches by relevance or date; there is no advanced search. The sort option appears on the right of the results page as you search.

International Versions

In addition to the primarily U.S.-focused Google News site, Google's begun rolling out country-specific news pages. At the time of this writing, there are pages for Australia (*http://news.google.com.au*), Canada (*http://news.google.ca*), India (*http://news.google.com/india*), the U.K. (*http://news.google.co.uk*), and New Zealand (*http://news.google.com.nz*). For a consummate list, see the "International versions of Google News available in:" links at the bottom of the main Google News page.

The country-specific news sites do not appear to have different news story indexes. Rather, the front page of each focuses on the particular country's current news. Each page does, however, have a link to news specific to that country in the lefthand navigation bar.

These country-specific news pages are good for focusing your news browsing and for getting a sense of what sources Google uses for different countries.

Google News Special Syntax

Google News supports two special syntax elements.

intitle:

intitle: finds words in the article headline.

```
intitle:miners
```

source:

source: restricts your query to stories coming from a particular news source.

```
miners site:bbc.co.uk
```

If you search for cricket source:bbc, stories will be returned only if they come from the BBC. What happens if you want to search for a source that has multiple words? You separate the words with an underscore. Thus Washington Post becomes:

```
source:washington_post
```

Unfortunately, Google News does not offer a list of its more than 4,500 sources, so you have to guess a little when you're looking around.

Making the Most of Google News

The best thing about Google News is its clustering capabilities. On an ordinary news search engine, a breaking news story can overwhelm search results. For example, in late July 2002, a story broke that hormone replacement therapy might increase the risk of cancer. Suddenly, using a news search engine to find the phrase "breast cancer" was an exercise in futility, because dozens of stories around the same topic were clogging the results page.

That doesn't happen when you search the Google News engine, because Google groups cluster stories by topic. You'd find a large cluster of stories about hormone replacement therapy, but they'd be in one place, leaving you to find other news about breast cancer.

Does this always work perfectly? In my experience, no. Some searches cluster easily; they're specialized or tend to spawn limited topics. But other queries—like "George Bush"— spawn loads of results and several different clusters. If you need to search for a famous name or a general topic (like crime, for example) narrow your search results in one of the following ways:

- Add a topic modifier that will significantly narrow your search results, as in: "George Bush" environment, crime arson.
- Limit your search with one of the special syntax elements, for example: intitle: "George Bush".
- Limit your search to a particular site. Be warned that, while this works well for a major breaking news story, you might miss local stories. If you're searching for a major American story, CNN (site:cnn.com) is a good choice. If the story you're researching is more international in origin, the BBC (site:bbc.co.uk) works well.

If your searches are narrow or relatively obscure, the clustering issue may never come up for you. In that case, you won't

---

get to take advantage of Google's greatest strength and will instead notice its weaknesses: inability to search by date, inability to sort by source, limitations on searching by language or source, etc. In that case, you might want to try an alternative.

Beyond Google for News Search

After a long dry spell, news search engines have popped up all over the Internet. Here are a few favorites:

FAST News Search (http://www.alltheweb.com/?cat=news)
Great for both local and international sources. Advanced search lets you narrow your search by language, news source category (business, sports, etc.), and date the material was indexed. FAST's one drawback is that it has little press-release indexing.

Rocketinfo (http://www.rocketnews.com/)
Does not use the most extensive sources in the world, but lesser-known press-release outlets (like PETA) and very technical outlets (like OncoLink, BioSpace, Insurance News Net) are found here. Rocketinfo's main drawback is its limited search and sort options.

Yahoo! Daily News (http://dailynews.yahoo.com)
Sports its source list right on the advanced search page. A 30-day index means that sometimes you can find things that have slipped off the other engines. It also provides free news alerts for registered Yahoo! users. One drawback is that Yahoo! Daily News has few technical sources, which means that sometimes stories appear over and over in search results.

Google Catalogs

At the start of the dot-com boom, all the retailers rushed to put their catalogs online. Google sauntered along and long after all the hoopla has died down, it has put up catalogs in a different way. Instead of designing a web site that looks like a catalog, Google simply scanned in pages from catalogs—just under 6,000 of them at the time of this writing—and made them available via a search engine. Figure 21 gives you some idea of the diversity available.

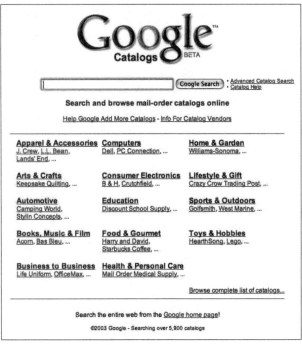

Figure 21. Google Catalogs

From the front page of Google Catalogs (located at *http://catalogs.google.com*), you can either do a simple keyword search or browse through a subject index of catalogs. Each catalog listing gives you the option to view the catalog, view previous editions, or link to the catalog's site (if available).

Figure 22 shows the top few results for a search for seattle mariners baseball merchandise.

Figure 22. Google Catalogs search results

If you choose to browse the catalog, as shown in Figure 23, you'll be provided an interface to page through, zoom, jump to a particular page, and a search bar at the right of the page for searching just that catalog.

If you're interested in a particular class of item (like electronics or toys or whatever), stick with the topical catalog browsing. If you're searching for a particular item, use the keyword search on the front page. If your search is somewhere in between, use the advanced search page.

The Advanced Catalog Search (*http://catalogs.google.com/advanced_catalog_search*) lets you narrow down your search by categories (from Apparel & Accessories to Toys & Hobbies), specify if you want to search only current catalogs or

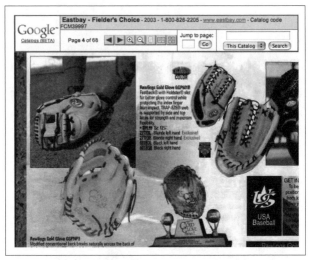

Figure 23. Browsing Google Catalogs

all past and current catalogs, and specify if you'd prefer to filter results using SafeSearch.

Google Catalogs' search results are very different from other Google properties. They include the catalog name and issue date, a picture of the catalog's front page, the first page where your search term appears (a link to additional results with your search term, if any, appears on the line with the name and date of the catalog), and a close-up of where your search term appears on the page. Generally, the pages in the search results aren't very readable, but that varies depending on the catalog. Click on the page to get a larger version of the entire page.

Google Catalogs Special Syntax

Google Catalogs does not have any special search syntax.

Froogle

Google Catalogs is a great way to do offline shopping, especially if you like to browse with nothing more than a couple of keywords. However, if you're the modern type who insists on doing all shopping online, you'll want to check out Froogle (*http://froogle.google.com/*).

"Froogle," a combination of the words "Google" and "frugal," is a searchable shopping index that looks a lot like the Google Directory (see Figure 24) with a focus on getting you right to an online point of purchase for the item you're interested in. The service was launched in December 2002 and, at the time of this writing, is still in beta.

Figure 24. Froogle

There are two ways of finding items in the Froogle directory: browsing and searching. In the same way as browsing and searching Google can lead to different results, so too will you find different products depending on the road you take in Froogle.

Browsing for Purchases

The Froogle home page lists a set of top-level categories, each with a representative smattering of subcategories. To browse a particular category, just click on the link. You'll find that even after some drilling down to just the subcategory you're after, there are still bound to be a lot of items. For example, there are currently over 3,000 results on the Flowers > Arrangement category.

Listings include a picture (when one is available, as is most often the case), price, the store selling the item, a brief description of the item, and a link leading to all items from that particular vendor in the category at hand. You can narrow things down by choosing to view only items within a particular price range.

Unless you have a lot of time and really like shopping, the browsing option is less than optimal. Searching Froogle works much better, especially when you're in a hurry and have something specific in mind.

Searching for Purchases

Froogle sports a basic keyword search, but to get the most out of your search, you want the Froogle Advanced Search (*http://froogle.google.com/froogle_advanced_search*).

Some of the Advanced Search will look familiar if you've used the standard Google Advanced Search; you can specify words, phrases, and words that should be excluded. But you can also specify products that are below a specified price or within a particular price range. You can also specify whether your keywords should appear within the product name, the product description, or both; this gives you some nice additional fine-grained control. Finally, you can specify the

---

category in which your results should appear from Apparel & Accessories to Toys & Games.

Figure 25 shows a sample set of Froogle search results.

Figure 25. Froogle search results

Froogle Special Syntax

Froogle does have some special syntax up its sleeve.

intitle:

intitle: restricts results by the name of the product.

```
intitle:giraffe
intitle:grundig porsche radio
```

intext:

intext: restricts results by the product description.

```
intext:figurine
intext:"short wave"
```

You can use `intitle:` and `intext:` in combination, so `intitle:giraffe intext:figurine` will work as expected.

There's also an OR option, specified by a | (pipe). For example, to find a glass giraffe or elephant, you would search for: `glass (intitle:giraffe | intitle:elephant)`.

Adding a Merchant to Froogle

With Google's prominence in the regular search space, it's reasonable to expect that Froogle will quickly become a popular shopping destination. If you sell things online, you might be wondering how much Google charges a vendor to be a part of the Froogle stable.

The short answer is: nothing! Yup, you can be listed in Froogle without paying a dime. There are some limitations, though. Currently, Froogle accepts only English-language web sites and products priced in U.S. dollars.

Merchants who wish to be included on the site are invited to submit a *data feed*—a tab-delimited file generated by your favorite spreadsheet program, in-house content management system, product database, or the like. For more information on making your products available via Froogle, see *http://froogle.google.com/froogle/merchants.html*.

Language Tools

In the early days of the Web, it seemed like most web pages were in English. But as more and more countries have come online, materials have become available in a variety of languages—including languages that don't originate with a particular country (such as Esperanto and Klingon).

Google offers several language tools, including one for translation and one for Google's interface. The interface option is much more extensive than the translation option, but the translation has a lot to offer.

Getting to the Language Tools

The Language Tools are available by clicking "Language Tools" on the front page or by going to *http://www.google. com/language_tools*.

The first tool, shown in Figure 26, allows you to search for materials from a certain country and/or in a certain language. This is an excellent way to narrow your searches; searching for French pages from Japan gives you far fewer results than searching for French pages from France. You can narrow the search further by searching for a slang word in another language. For example, search for the English slang word "yuppy" on French pages from Japan.

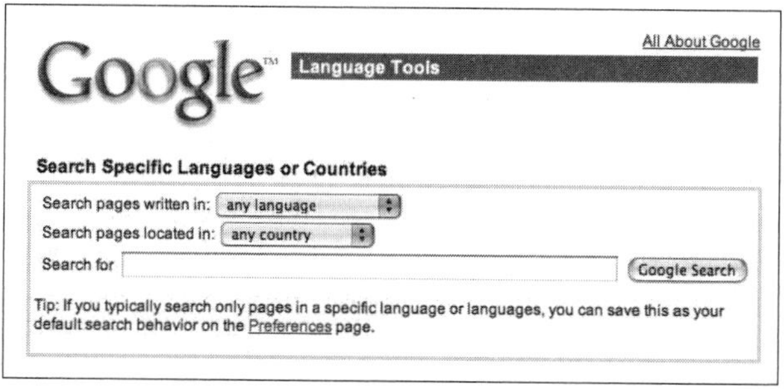

Figure 26. Google Language Tools

The second tool on this page (as seen in Figure 27) allows you to translate either a block of text or an entire web page from one language to another. Most of the translations are to or from English.

Machine translation is not nearly as good as human translation, so don't rely on this translation as either the basis of a search or as a completely accurate translation of the page you're looking at. Rely on it instead to give you the gist of whatever it translates.

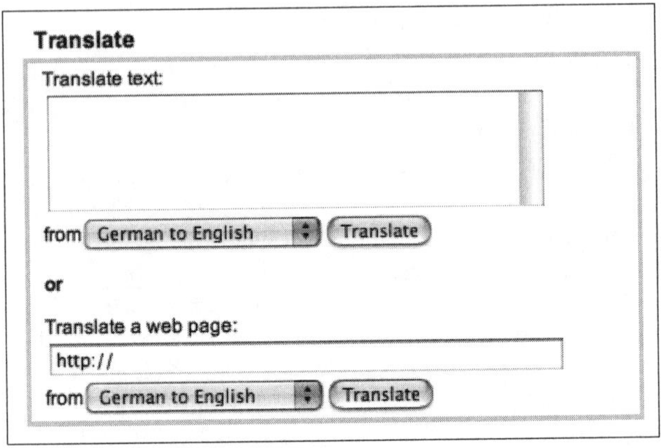

Figure 27. Google Translate tool

You don't have to come to this page to use the translation tools. When you enter a search, you'll see that some search results that aren't in your language of choice (which you set via Google's preferences) have "[Translate this page]" next to their titles. Click on one of those and you'll be presented with a framed, translated version of the page. The Google frame, at the top, gives you the option of viewing the original version of the page, as well as returning to the results or viewing a copy suitable for printing.

The third tool (see Figure 28) lets you choose the interface language for Google, from Afrikaans to Zulu. Some of these languages are imaginary (such as Bork, bork, bork! and Elmer Fudd), but they do work.

Be warned: if you set your language preference to Klingon, you'll need to know Klingon to figure out how to set it back. If you're really stuck, delete the Google cookie from your browser and reload the page; this should reset all preferences to the defaults.

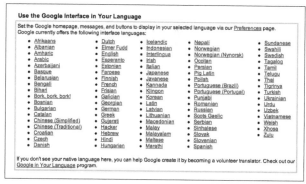

Figure 28. Google in Your Language

How does Google manage to have so many interface languages when they have so few translation languages? Because of the Google in Your Language program, which gathers volunteers from around the world to translate Google's interface. (You can get more information on that program at *http://www.google.com/intl/en/language.html*.)

Finally, the Language Tools page contains a list of region-specific Google home pages—over 30 of them, from Deutschland to Pitcairn Islands. Figure 29 shows just a few.

Making the Most of Google's Language Tools

While you shouldn't rely on Google's translation tools to give you more than the gist of the meaning (machine translation isn't that good), you can use translations to narrow your searches. The first way I described earlier: use unlikely combinations of languages and countries to narrow your results. The second way involves using the translator.

Select a word that matches your topic and use the translator to translate it into another language. (Google's translation tools work very well for single-word translations like this.) Now, search for that word in a country and language that don't match it. For example, you might search for the

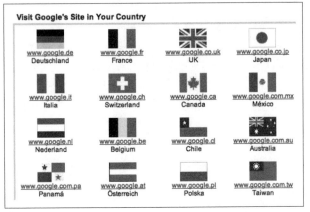

Figure 29. Google's Site in Your Country

German word "Landstraße" (highway) on French pages in Canada. Of course, you'll have to be sure to use words that don't have English equivalents or you'll be overwhelmed with results.

Consulting the Dictionary

Google's own spellchecking (see "Checking Spelling" in Part III) is built upon its own word and phrase database gleaned while indexing web pages. Thus, it provides suggestions for lesser-known proper names, phrases, common sentence constructs, etc. Google also offers a definition service powered by Dictionary.com (*http://www.dictionary.com*). Definitions, while coming from a credible source and augmented by various specialty indexes, can be more limited.

Run a search. You'll notice on the results page the phrase "Searched the web for [query words]." If the query words appear in a dictionary, they will be hyperlinked to a dictionary definition. Identified phrases will be linked as a phrase; for example, the query "jolly roger" will allow you to look up the phrase "jolly roger." On the other hand, the phrase "computer legal" will allow you to look up the separate words "computer" and "legal."

The definition search will sometimes fail on obscure words, very new words, slang, and technical vocabularies (otherwise known as specialized slang). If you search for a word's meaning and Google can't help you, try enlisting the services of a metasearch dictionary like OneLook (*http://www.onelook.com*), which indexes over 4 million words in over 700 dictionaries. If that doesn't work, try Google again with one of the following tricks:

- If you're searching for several words—you're reading a technical manual, for example—search for several of the words at the same time. Sometimes you'll find a glossary this way. For example, maybe you're reading a book about marketing, and you don't know many of the words. If you search for storyboard stet SAU, you'll get only a few search results, and they'll all be glossaries.

- Try searching for your word and the word glossary; say, stet glossary. Be sure to use an unusual word; you may not know what a "spread" is in the context of marketing, but searching for spread glossary will get you over 300,000 results for many different kinds of glossaries.

- Try searching for the phrase *queryword* means or the words What does *queryword* mean?, where *queryword* is the word you want to find.

- If you're searching for a medical or a technical item, narrow your search to educational (*.edu*) sites. If you want a contextual definition for using equine acupuncture and how it might be used to treat laminitis, try site:edu "equine acupuncture" laminitis.

- site:edu will give you a brief list of results. Furthermore, you'll avoid book lists and online stores, which is handy if you're seeking information and don't necessarily want to purchase anything. If you're searching for slang, try narrowing your search to sites like Geocities and Tripod, and see what happens. Sometimes young people put fan sites and other informal cultural collections up on free places like Geocities, and using these you can find many examples of slang in context instead of dry lists of definitions. There is an amazing number of glossaries on Geocities; search for glossary site:geocities.com, and see for yourself.

Google's connection with Dictionary.com means that simple definition checking is very fast and easy. But even more obscure words can be found quickly if you apply a little creative thinking.

Consulting the Phonebook

Google combines residential and business phone-number information and its own excellent interface to offer a phonebook lookup that provides listings for businesses and residences in the United States. However, the search offers three different syntax elements, different levels of information provide different results, the syntax elements are finicky, and Google doesn't provide any documentation.

Google Phonebook Special Syntax

Google offers three ways to search its phonebook.

phonebook:

phonebook: searches the entire Google phonebook.

    phonebook: lucky Las Vegas NV

rphonebook:

rphonebook: searches residential listings only.

    rphonebook: Smith CA

bphonebook:

bphonebook: searches business listings only.

```
bphonebook: pizza Chicago IL
```

NOTE

The results page for phonebook: lookups lists only 5 residential and 5 business results combined. The more specific rphonebook: and bphonebook: searches provide up to 30 results per page. For a better chance of finding what you're looking for, use the appropriate targeted lookup.

Using a standard phonebook requires knowing quite a bit of information about what you're looking for: first name, last name, city, and state. Google's phonebook requires no more than last name and state to get it started. Casting a wide net for all the Smiths in California is as simple as:

```
phonebook:smith ca
```

Try giving 411 a whirl with that request! Figure 30 shows the results of this query.

Figure 30. A phonebook: results page

Notice that, while intuition might tell you there are thousands of Smiths in California, the Google phonebook says there are only 600. Just as Google's regular search engine maxes out at 1,000 results, its phonebook maxes out at 600. Fair enough. Try narrowing down your search by adding a first name, city, or both:

```
phonebook:john smith los angeles ca
```

At the time of this writing, the Google phonebook finds 3 business and 22 residential listings for John Smith in Los Angeles, California.

Caveats. The phonebook syntax elements are powerful and useful, but they can be difficult to use if you don't remember a few things about how they work:

- They are case-sensitive. Searching for phonebook:john doe ca works, while Phonebook:john doe ca (notice the capital P) doesn't.

- Wildcards don't work. Then again, they're not needed; the Google phonebook does all the wildcarding for you. For example, if you want to find shops in New York with "coffee" in the title, don't bother trying to envision every permutation of "Coffee Shop," "Coffee House," and so on. Just search for bphonebook:coffee new york ny and you'll get a list of any business in New York whose name contains the word "coffee. "

- Exclusions don't work. Perhaps you want to find coffee shops that aren't Starbucks. You might think phonebook:coffee -starbucks new york ny would do the trick. After all, you're searching for coffee and not Starbucks, right? Unfortunately not; Google thinks you're looking for both the words "coffee" and "starbucks," yielding just the opposite of what you were hoping for: everything Starbucks in NYC.

- OR doesn't work on city or state. You might start wondering if Google's phonebook accepts OR lookups. You then might experiment, trying to find all the coffee shops in

Rhode Island or Hawaii: `bphonebook:coffee (ri | hi)`. Unfortunately that doesn't work; the only listings you'll get are for coffee shops in Hawaii. That's because Google is paying attention only to the right-most letters, treating them as location, in this case, Hawaii (hi). You can, however, use the OR syntax in the rest of the query, as long as you specify the state at the end (far right). For example, if you want to find coffee shops that sell either donuts or bagels in Massachusetts, this query works fine: `bphonebook:coffee (donuts | bagels) ma`. It finds stores that contain the word "coffee" and either the word "donuts" or the word "bagels" in Massachusetts. The bottom line: you can use an OR query on the business's or person's name, but not on the location.

Reverse phonebook lookup. All three phonebook syntax elements support reverse lookup, though it's probably best to use the general `phonebook:` syntax to avoid not finding what you are looking for due to its residential or business classification.

To do a reverse search, just enter the phone number with area code. Lookups without area code won't work.

```
phonebook:(707) 829-0515
```

Note that reverse lookups on Google are a hit-or-miss proposition and don't always produce results. If you're not having any luck, you may wish to use a more dedicated phonebook site like WhitePages.com (*http://www.whitepages.com/*).

NOTE

If you're concerned about privacy, you can have Google remove your phonebook listing. Visit *http://www.google.com/help/pbremoval.html* for more information.

Finding phonebooks using Google. While Google's phonebook is a good starting point, its usefulness is limited. If you're looking for a phone number at a university or other large institution, while you won't find the number in Google, you certainly can find the appropriate phonebook if it's online.

If you're looking for a university phonebook, try this simple search first: inurl:phone site:*university.edu*, replacing *university.edu* with the domain of the university you're looking for. For example, to find the online phonebook of the University of North Carolina at Chapel Hill, you'd search for:

```
inurl:phone site:unc.edu
```

If that doesn't work, there are several variations you can try, again substituting your preferred university's domain for *unc.edu*:

```
title:"phone book" site:unc.edu

(phonebook | "phone book") lookup faculty staff site:unc.edu

inurl:help (phonebook | "phone book") site:unc.edu
```

If you're looking for several university phonebooks, try the same search with the more generic site:edu rather than a specific university's domain. There are also a couple of web sites that list university phonebooks:

- Phonebook Gateway–Server Lookup (*http://www.uiuc.edu/cgi-bin/ph/lookup*) has over 330 phonebooks.
- Phone Book Servers (*http://www.envmed.rochester.edu/www/ph.html*) has over 400 phonebooks.

Tracking Stocks

Among the lesser-known pantheon of Google syntax is stocks:. Searching for stocks:*symbol*, where *symbol* represents the stock you're looking for, will redirect you to Yahoo! Finance (*http://finance.yahoo.com*) for details. The Yahoo! page is actually framed by Google; off to the top-left is the Google logo, along with links to Quicken, Fool.com, MSN MoneyCentral, and other financial sites.

Feed Google a bum stock: query and you'll still find your-self at Yahoo! Finance, usually staring at a quote for a stock you've never even heard of or a "Stock Not Found" page. Of course, you can use this to your advantage. Enter stocks:, followed by the name of a company you're looking for (e.g., stocks:friendly). If the company's name is more than one word, choose the most unique word. Run your query and you'll arrive at the Yahoo! Finance stock lookup page, shown in Figure 31.

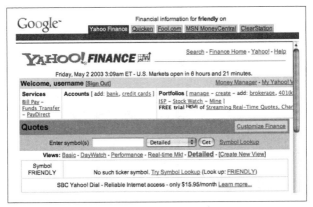

Figure 31. Yahoo! Finance stock lookup page

Notice the "Look up: FRIENDLY" link; click it and you'll be offered a list of companies that match "friendly" in some way. From there you can get the stock information you want (assuming the company you wanted is on the list).

Beyond Google for Basic Stock Information

Google isn't particularly set up for basic stock research. You'll have to do your initial groundwork elsewhere, return-ing to Google armed with a better understanding of what you're looking for. I recommend going straight to Yahoo! Finance (*http://finance.yahoo.com*) to quickly look up stocks by symbol or company name; there you'll find all the basics: quotes, company profiles, charts, and recent news. For more in-depth coverage, I heartily recommend Hoovers (*http:// www.hoovers.com*). Some of the information is free. For more depth, you'll have to pay a subscription fee.

More Stock Research with Google

Try searching Google for:

    "Tootsie Roll"

Now add the stock symbol, TR, to your query:

    "Tootsie Roll" TR

Aha! Instantly the search results shift to financial information. Now, add the name of the CEO:

    "Tootsie Roll" TR "Melvin Gordon"

You'll end up with a nice, small, targeted list of results, as shown in Figure 32.

Figure 32. Using a stock symbol to limit results

Stock symbols are great "fingerprints" for Internet research. They're consistent, they often appear along with the company name, and they're unusal enough that they do a nice job of narrowing down your search results to relevant information.

There are also several words and phrases you can use to narrow down your search for company-related information. Replacing *company* with the name of the company you're looking for, try these:

- For press releases: "*company* announced", "*company* announces", "*company* reported".
- For financial information: *company* "quarterly report", *company* SEC, *company* financials, *company* "p/e ratio".
- For location information: *company* parking airport location doesn't always work, but sometimes works amazingly well.

Searching Article Archives

Not all sites have their own search engines, and even the ones that do are sometimes difficult to use. Complicated or incomplete search engines are more pain than gain when you're attempting to search through archives of published articles. If you follow a couple of rules, Google is handy for finding back issues of published resources.

The trick is to use a common phrase to find the information you're looking for. Let's use *The New York Times* as an example.

Articles from The New York Times

Your first intuition when searching for previously published articles from NYTimes.com might be to simply use site: nytimes.com in your Google query. For example, if I wanted to find articles on George Bush, why not use:

```
"george bush" site:nytimes.com
```

This will indeed find you all articles mentioning George Bush published on NYTimes.com. What it won't find is all the articles produced by *The New York Times* but republished elsewhere.

NOTE

While doing research, keep credibility firmly in mind. If you're doing casual research, maybe you don't need to double-check a story to make sure it actually comes from *The New York Times*, but if you're researching a term paper, doublecheck the veracity of every article you find that isn't actually on *The New York Times* site.

What you actually want is a clear identifier, no matter the site of origin, that an article comes from *The New York Times*. Copyright notices are perfect for the job. A copyright notice for *The New York Times* typically reads:

```
Copyright 2001 The New York Times Company
```

Of course, this would only find articles from 2001. A simple workaround is to replace the year with a Google full-word wildcard:

```
Copyright * The New York Times Company
```

Let's try that George Bush search again, this time using the snippet of copyright notice instead of the `site:` restriction:

```
"Copyright *  The New York Times Company" "George Bush"
```

At the time of this writing, you get over three times as many results for this search than you get using the earlier attempt.

Magazine Articles

Copyright notices are also useful for finding magazine articles. For example, *Scientific American*'s typical copyright notice looks like this:

```
Scientific American, Inc. All rights reserved.
```

(The date appears before the company name, so I just dropped it to avoid having to bother with wildcards.)

Using that copyright notice as a quote-delimited phrase along with a search word—hologram, for example—yields the Google query:

```
hologram "Scientific American, Inc. All rights reserved."
```

At the time of this writing, you'll get one result, which seems like a small number for a general query like hologram. When you get fewer results than you expect, fall back on using the site: syntax to go back to the originating site itself:

```
hologram site:sciam.com
```

In this example, you'll find several results that you can grab from Google's cache but that are no longer available on the Scientific American site.

Most publications that I've come across have some kind of common text string that you can use when searching Google for its archives. Usually it's a copyright notice and most often it's at the bottom of a page. Use Google to search for that string and whatever query words you're interested in. If that doesn't work, fall back on searching for the query string and domain name.

Finding Directories of Information

Sometimes you're more interested in large information collections than scouring for specific bits and bobs. Using Google, there are a couple of ways to find directories, link lists, and other information collections. The first way makes use of Google's full-word wildcards and the intitle: syntax. The second is judicious use of particular keywords.

Title Tags and Wildcards

Pick something you'd like to find collections of information about. We'll use "trees" as our example. The first thing we'll look for is any page with the words "directory" and "trees" in its title. In fact, we'll use a couple of full-word wildcards (* characters) to build in a little buffering for words that might appear between the two. The resultant query looks something like this:

```
intitle:"directory * * trees"
```

This query will find directories of evergreen trees, South African trees, and, of course, directories containing simply garden variety "trees."

What if you wanted to take things up a notch, taxonomically speaking, and find directories of botanical information? You'd use a combination of intitle: and keywords, like so:

```
botany intitle:"directory of"
```

And you'd get over 6,600 results. Changing the tenor of the information might be a matter of restricting results to those coming from academic institutions. Appending an "edu" site specification brings you to:

```
botany intitle:"directory of" site:edu
```

This gets you around 120 results, a mixture of resource directories and, unsurprisingly, directories of university professors.

Mixing this syntax works rather well when you're searching for something that might also be an offline print resource. For example:

```
cars intitle:"encyclopedia of"
```

This query pulls in results from Amazon.com and other sites selling car encyclopedias. Filter out some of the more obvious results by tweaking the query slightly:

```
cars intitle:"encyclopedia of" -site:amazon.com ⏎
-inurl:book -inurl:products
```

This query specifies that search results should not come from Amazon.com and should not have the words "book" or "products" in the URL, which eliminates a fair amount of online stores. Play with this query by changing the word "cars" to whatever you'd like for some interesting finds.

(Of course there are lots of sites selling books online, but when it comes to injecting "noise" into results when you're trying to find online resources and research-oriented information, Amazon.com is the biggest offender. If you're actually looking for books, try site:amazon.com instead.)

If mixing syntax doesn't do the trick for the resources you want, there are some clever keyword combinations that might just do the trick.

Finding Searchable Subject Indexes

There are a few major searchable subject indexes and myriad minor ones that deal with a particular topic or idea. You can find the smaller subject indexes by customizing a few generic searches. "what's new" "what's cool" directory, while gleaning a few false results, is a great way of finding searchable subject indexes. directory "gossamer threads" new is an interesting one. Gossamer Threads is the creator of a popular link-directory program. This is a good way to find searchable subject indexes without too many false hits. directory "what's new" categories cool doesn't work particularly well, because the word "directory" is not a very reliable search term, but you will pull in some things with this query that you might otherwise miss.

Let's put a few of these into practice:

```
"what's new" "what's cool" directory phylum
"what's new" "what's cool" directory carburetor
"what's new" "what's cool" directory "investigative ⏎
journalism"
"what's new" directory categories gardening
directory "gossamer threads" new sailboats
directory "what's new" categories cool "basset hounds"
```

The real trick is to use a more general word, but make it unique enough that it applies mostly to your topic and not to many other topics.

Take acupuncture, for instance. Start narrowing it down by topic: what kind of acupuncture? For people or animals? If for people, what kind of conditions are being treated? If for animals, what kind of animals? Maybe you should be searching for "cat acupuncture" or maybe you should be searching for acupuncture arthritis. If this first round doesn't narrow down search results enough for you, keep going. Are you looking for education or treatment? You can skew results one way or the other by using the site: syntax. Maybe you want "cat acupuncture" site:com or arthritis acupuncture site: edu. Just by taking a few steps to narrow things down, you can get a reasonable number of search results focused around your topic.

Finding Technical Definitions

Specialized vocabularies remain, for the most part, fairly static; words don't suddenly change their meaning all that often. Not so with technical and computer-related jargon. It seems like every 12 seconds someone comes up with a new buzzword or term relating to computers or the Internet, and then 12 minutes later it becomes obsolete or means something completely different—often more than one thing at a time. Maybe it's not that bad. It just feels that way.

Google can help you in two ways: by helping you look up words and by helping you figure out what words you don't know that you need to know.

Technology Terminology

You just got out of the conference room and so many new words were slung at you your head is buzzing. The problem at this point is that you don't know if you've been hearing slang, hardware/software-specific terminology, or general terminology. How do you determine which is which?

As with any new vocabulary, you're going to have to use contextual clues. In what part of the conversation was the term

---

used? Was it used most often in relation to something? Did only one person use the term? It might just be slang. Is it written down anywhere? Try to get all the information about it that you can. If there is no information about it available—for example, if your boss stuck her head in your cubicle and said, "We're thinking of spending $20 million on a project using X. What do you think?"—treat it as general terminology.

Google Glossary

Before you start your search at Google, check and see whether Google Labs is still offering the Google Glossary (*http://labs.google.com/glossary/*).

NOTE

Google Labs is a place where Google engineers make experimental services available to the public; find out more about Google Labs in *Google Hacks*, Hack #35, or at *http://labs.google.com/faq.html*.

The Google Glossary provides definitions of both technical and nontechnical terms. If that doesn't turn up anything useful, move on to Google.

Researching Terminology with Google

First things first: for heaven's sake, please don't just plug the abbreviation into the query box! For example, searching for XSLT will net you 900,000 results. While combing through the sites Google turns up may eventually lead you to a definition, there's more to life than that. Instead, add "stands for" to the query if it's an abbreviation or acronym.

"XSLT stands for" returns around 29 results, and the very first is a tutorial glossary. If you're still getting too many results ("XML stands for" gives you almost 1,000 results), try adding beginners or newbie to the query. "XML stands for" beginners brings in 35 results, the first being "XML for beginners."

If you're still not getting the results you want, try "What is X?" or "X is short for" or X beginners FAQ, where X is the acronym or term. These should be regarded as second-tier methods, because most sites don't tend to use phrases like "What is X?" on their pages, "X is short for" is uncommon language usage, and X might be so new (or so obscure) that it doesn't yet have a FAQ entry. Then again, your mileage may vary and it's worth a shot; there's a lot of terminology out there.

If you have hardware- or software-specific terminology—as opposed to just hardware- or software-related—try the word or phrase along with anything you might know about its usage. For example, "DynaLoader" is software-specific terminology; it's a Perl module. That much known, simply give the two words a spin:

```
DynaLoader Perl
```

If the results you're finding are too advanced and assume you already know what a DynaLoader is, start playing with the words beginners, newbie, and the like to bring you closer to information for beginners:

```
DynaLoader Perl Beginners
```

If you still can't find the word in Google, there are a few possible causes: perhaps it's slang specific to your area, your coworkers are playing with your mind, you heard it wrong (or there was a typo on the printout you got), or it's very, very new.

Where to Go When It's Not on Google

Despite your best efforts, you're not finding good explanations of the terminology on Google. There are a few other sites that might have what you're looking for:

Whatis (http://whatis.techtarget.com/)
A searchable subject index of computer terminology, from software to telecom. This is especially useful if you have a hardware- or software-specific word, because the definitions are divided into categories. You can also browse alphabetically. Annotations are good and are often cross-indexed.

Webopedia (http://www.pcwebopaedia.com/)
Searchable by keyword or browseable by category. This site also has a list of the newest entries on the front page, so you can check for new words.

Netlingo (http://www.netlingo.com/framesindex.html)
This site is more Internet-oriented. It shows up with a frame on the left containing the words, with the definitions on the right. It includes lots of cross-referencing and really old slang.

Tech Encyclopedia (http://www.techweb.com/encyclopedia/)
Features definitions and information on over 20,000 words. The top 10 terms searched for are listed, so you can see if everyone else is as confused as you are. Though entries have before-the-listing and after-the-listing lists of words, there is only moderate cross-referencing.

Geek terminology proliferates almost as quickly as web pages. Don't worry too much about deliberately keeping up—it's just about impossible. Instead, use Google as a "ready reference" resource for definitions.

Finding Weblog Commentary

There was a time that you needed to find current commentary, you didn't turn to a full-text search engine like Google. You searched Usenet, combed mailing lists, or searched through current news sites like CNN.com and hoped for the best.

But as search engines have evolved, they've been able to index pages more quickly than once every few weeks. In fact, Google tunes its engine to more readily index sites with a high information churn rate. At the same time, a phenomenon called the weblog (see *Essential Blogging, http://www. oreilly.com/catalog/essblogging*) has arisen: an online site that keeps a running commentary and associated links, updated daily—and, indeed, even more often in many cases. Google indexes many of these sites on an accelerated schedule. If you know how to find them, you can build a query that searches just these sites for recent commentary.

Finding Weblogs

When weblogs first appeared on the Internet, they were generally updated manually or by using homemade programs. Thus, there were no standard words you could add to a search engine to find them. Now, however, many weblogs are created using either specialized software packages (like Movable Type, *http://www.movabletype.org*, or Radio Userland, *http://radio.userland.com*) or as online services (like Blogger, *http://www.blogger.com*). These programs and services are more easily found online with some clever use of special syntax or magic words.

For hosted weblogs, the site: syntax makes things easy. Blogger weblogs that are hosted at Blog*Spot (*http://www. blogspot.com*) can be found using site: blogspot.com. Even though Radio Userland is a software program that is able to post its weblogs to any web server, you can find the majority of Radio Userland weblogs at the Radio Userland community server (*http://radio.weblogs.com/*) using site:radio. weblogs.com.

Finding weblogs powered by weblog software and hosted elsewhere is more problematic; Movable Type weblogs, for example, can be found all over the Internet. However, most of them sport a "powered by movable type" link of some sort; therefore, searching for the phrase "powered by movable type" will find many of them.

It comes down to "magic words" typically found on weblog pages—shout-outs, if you will, to the software or hosting sites. The following list provides some of these packages and services and the magic words used to find them in Google:

Blogger
    "powered by blogger" or site:blogspot.com

Blosxom
    "powered by blosxom"

Greymatter
    "powered by greymatter"

Geeklog
    "powered by geeklog"

Manila
    "a manila site" or site:editthispage.com

Pitas (a service)
    site:pitas.com

pMachine
    "powered by pmachine"

uJournal (a service)
    site:ujournal.org

LiveJournal (a service)
    site:livejournal.com

Radio Userland
    intitle:"radio weblog" or site:radio.weblogs.com

Using the "Magic Words"

Because you can't have more than 10 words in a Google query, there's no way to build a query that includes every conceivable weblog's magic words. It's best to experiment with the various words and see which weblogs have the materials you're interested in.

First of all, realize that weblogs are usually informal commentary and you'll have to keep an eye out for misspelled words, names, etc. Generally, it's better to search by event than by name, if possible. For example, if you were looking for commentary on a potential strike, the phrase "baseball strike" would be a better search, initially, than a search for the name of the Commissioner of Major League Baseball, Bud Selig.

You can also try to search for a word or phrase relevant to the event. For example, for a baseball strike you could try searching for "baseball strike" "red sox" (or "baseball strike" bosox). If you're searching for information on a wildfire and wondering if anyone was arrested for arson, try wildfire arrested and, if that doesn't work, wildfire arrested arson. (Why not search for arson to begin with? Because it's not certain that a weblog commentator would use the word "arson." Instead, he might just refer to someone being arrested for setting the fire. "Arrested" in this case is a more certain word than "arson.")

The Google Toolbar

Unlike many search engines, Google never became a "portal"; that is, it did not try to provide all information to all people as well as put ads on every square inch of its web site.

Because of that, it was never important that Google get people to its front page; all its ads are on its pages of search results. So it made sense that Google was able to offer the Google Toolbar™.

The Google Toolbar is an add-on, currently available only for Internet Explorer, that offers all the functionality of the Google site without having to visit the site itself. In fact, the

Google Toolbar offers more functionality; it's the only way you can see exactly what a site's PageRank is.

You can download the Google Toolbar for free at *http:// toolbar.google.com*. You need Internet Explorer with ActiveX functions enabled to download and install the toolbar.

Once installed, the Google Toolbar actively keeps track of what you're viewing and asks Google (by passing on the URL) for anything it knows about the page, including Page-Rank and categorization. Some people might be concerned that Google could misuse the information being sent, so Google offers the option of installing the toolbar without the PageRank features, which protects your privacy. If you don't know which you want to do, go ahead and choose the complete download. You can always disable the PageRank and Category tools later using the toolbar options. The installed toolbar is shown in Figure 33.

Figure 33. The Google Toolbar

Using the toolbar for Web search is simple: enter some text in the query box and hit Enter. You'll get a page of Google results and some of the tools on the toolbar will light up. You'll be able to retrieve information about the returned page, move up one directory from the current page (in this case, it would move you to the Google home page), and use the highlight tool to highlight all occurrences of your search term in the document.

The toolbar works just as well when you're surfing using Internet Explorer's URL box. The Page Info button will give you the option of seeing a cached version of the page you're viewing (assuming Google has a cached version available), as well as showing backward links to the page, similar pages, and the opportunity to translate the page into English if it isn't already in English. Generally speaking, the more popular a page is, the more likely it is to have backward links and similar pages.

But where are all the other offerings, such as the Image search, the Catalog search, and the Google Groups search? They're available, but the default install of the Google Toolbar turns them off. Click on the Google logo on the left side of the toolbar and choose Toolbar Options.

You'll see that the Options page allows you to add several more search buttons, including the I'm Feeling Lucky button (that'll take you directly to Google's first search result), the Image search button, the Google Groups search button, and the Google Directory search button. If you feel like expressing your opinion, you can also activate the voting buttons; when you visit a page, you can click on the happy-face or sad-face button to express your opinion of the page.

If you're feeling adventurous, use the Experimental Features link at the bottom of the screen. This option will let you set up a Combined Search button. The Combined Search button looks like the Search Web button already on the toolbar, with a small triangle next to it. Click on the triangle and you'll get a drop-down menu that lets you search several Google properties, including images, Usenet, dictionary, stock quotes, and several of the specialty searches such as Linux, Apple Macintosh, and Microsoft.

NOTE

If you don't have Internet Explorer, you can get close with the Mozilla Toolbar (*http://googlebar.mozdev.org*) for the Mozilla browser or a newer version of Netscape Navigator (Version 7). If you don't use Mozilla, IE, or a Mozilla-based browser, try the browser-independent Quick Search Toolbar (*http://notesbydave.com/toolbar/doc.htm*).

Googling with Bookmarklets

You probably know what bookmarks are. But what are bookmarklets? Bookmarklets are like bookmarks but with an extra bit of JavaScript magic added. This makes them more interactive than regular bookmarks; they can perform small functions like opening a window, grabbing highlighted text from a web page, or submitting a query to a search engine. There are several bookmarklets that allow you to perform useful Google functions right from the comfort of your own browser.

NOTE

If you're using Internet Explorer for Windows, you're in gravy: all these bookmarklets will most likely work as advertised. But if you're using a less-appreciated browser (such as Opera) or operating system (such as Mac OS X), pay attention to the bookmarklet requirements and instructions; there may be special magic needed to get a particular bookmark working, or indeed, you may not be able to use the bookmarklet at all.

Before you try any other site, try Google's Browser Buttons (read: bookmarklets). Google Search queries Google for any text you've highlighted on the current web page. Google Scout performs a related: search on the current web page.

Google's bookmarklets are designed for the Internet Explorer browser:

Google Translate!
> Puts Google's translation tools (described earlier in "Language Tools") into a bookmarklet, enabling one-button translation of the current web page.
>
> *http://www.microcontentnews.com/resources/ ↵ translator.htm*

Google Jump

Prompts you for search terms, performs a Google search, and takes you straight to the top hit, thanks to the magic of Google's I'm Feeling Lucky function.

http://www.angelfire.com/dc/dcbookmarkletlab/ ↵
Bookmarklets/script002.html

The Dooyoo Bookmarklets Collection

Features several bookmarklets for use with different search engines—two for Google. Similar to Google's Browser Buttons, one finds highlighted text and the other finds related pages.

http://dooyoo-uk.tripod.com/bookmarklets2.html

Joe Maller's Translation Bookmarkets

Translate the current page into the specified language via Google or AltaVista.

http://www.joemaller.com/ ↵
translation_bookmarklets.shtml

Bookmarklets for Opera

Includes a Google translation bookmarklet, a Google bookmarklet that restricts searches to the current domain, and a bookmarklet that searches Google Groups (see "Google Groups"). As you might imagine, these bookmarklets were created for use with the Opera browser.

http://www.philburns.com/bookmarklets.html

GoogleIt!

Another bookmarklet that searches Google for any text you highlight on the current web page.

http://www.code9.com/googleit.html

PART V

Appendix

Syntax Summary

As well as the actual keywords you're asking for, Google has a rich set of search syntax elements. You can find more details about each and how to mix them effectively in Part II.

Phrase Search

Group words together to form phrases that must be found verbatim. The exact phrase must be found in a document for a match to be made.

```
"leading economic indicators"
```

Boolean AND/OR

By default, *all* the keywords you enter must exist for a match to be found. In other words, with:

```
snowblower Honda "Green Bay"
```

there's a Boolean AND that's implied. Use an OR (alternately, you can use a |, the pipe or vertical bar character) between each item:

```
snowblower OR snowmobile OR "Green Bay"
snowblower | snowmobile | "Green Bay"
```

if *any* of the words or phrases are sufficient for a match.

Parentheses

Use parentheses to group together a list of words that are alternatives in a search to suggest precedence, using the Boolean OR to separate them.

```
snowblower (snowmobile OR "Green Bay")
```

Explicit Inclusion

Use the + symbol in order to force stop words—short, common words that would otherwise be ignored—to be taken into account.

```
+in +and out
```

Negation

To specify that a word or phrase must *not* appear in your results, use a - (minus sign or dash).

```
snowblower snowmobile -"Green Bay"
```

Full-Word Wildcard

Use a full-word wildcard inside a quote-enclosed phrase to act as a substitute for one full word.

```
"three * mice"
```

will find "three blind mice", "three red mice", and so on.

intitle:

Restricts the search for the word to the titles of web pages.

```
intitle:"men's lacrosse"
```

allintitle:

Finds pages in which all the specified words appear in the title.

```
allintitle: "money supply" economics
```

intext:

Searches for the word in body text (ignores links text, URLs, and titles).

```
intext:http
```

allintext:

Finds pages where all the specified words appear in the page's body text.

```
allintext:html reference
```

inurl:

Restricts your search to the URLs of web pages.

```
inurl:help
```

allinurl:

Finds all the words listed in a URL.

```
allinurl:search help
```

inanchor:

Searches for text in a page's link anchors.

```
inanchor:"tom peters"
```

allinanchor:

Searches for all the words listed in a page's link anchors.

```
allinanchor:open source conference
```

site:

Narrows the search by either a site or a top-level domain.

```
site:co.uk
site:thomas.loc.gov
```

link:

Returns a list of pages linking to the specified URL.

```
link:www.google.com
```

cache:

Finds a copy of the page in Google's cache.

```
cache:www.yahoo.com
```

daterange:

Limits the search to a particular date or range of dates that a page was indexed (not when it was created).

```
neurosurgery daterange:2452389-2452389
"Geri Halliwell" "Spice Girls" daterange:2450958-2450968
```

filetype:

Restricts the search results to the file types you specify.

```
homeschooling filetype:pdf
"rfc 2616" filetype:txt
```

related:

Finds pages related to the specified page.

```
related:www.cnn.com
```

info:

Provides a page of links to more information about the specified URL.

```
info:www.oreilly.com
```

phonebook:

Looks up phone numbers.

```
phonebook:John Doe CA
phonebook:(510) 555-1212
```

rphonebook:

Looks up residential phonebook listings.

```
rphonebook:John Deere IL
```

bphonebook:

Looks up business phonebook listings.

```
bphonebook:John Deere IL
```

stocks:

Looks up stock information at Yahoo! Finance.

```
stocks: yhoo
stocks: apple
```

The latter—given that apple isn't an existing stock symbol—lands you on a Yahoo! Finance "Stock Not Found" page. From there, you can perform a stock symbol lookup, and find the correct symbol for Apple Computer—AAPL.

Julian Dates

While date-based searching is fantastically useful, date-based searching with Julian dates is annoying at best—for a human, anyway.

A Julian date is just one number. It's not broken up into month, day, and year. It's the number of days that have passed since January 1, 4713 B.C. Unlike Gregorian days (those on the calendar you and I use every day), which begin at midnight, Julian days begin at noon, making them useful for astronomers.

While problematic for humans, they're rather handy for computer programming, because to change dates you simply have to add and subtract from one number and not worry about month and year changes, not to mention leap years and the differing number of days in each month.

Google's daterange: special syntax element employs Julian dates.

NOTE

If things weren't confusing enough, there is actually another date format that is *also* known as a Julian Date format. It's a five-digit number, *yyddd*, where the first two digits represent the most significant digits of the year and the last three represent the day of the year, where the value is between 1 and 365 (or 366 in a leap year).

Google's daterange: syntax doesn't support the *yyddd* format.

There are plenty of places you can convert Julian dates online. We've found a couple of nice converters at the U.S. Naval Observatory Astronomical Applications Department (*http://aa.usno.navy.mil/data/docs/JulianDate.html*) and Mauro Orlandini's home page (*http://www.tesre.bo.cnr.it/~mauro/JD/*), the latter converting either Julian to Gregorian or vice versa. If you'd prefer to perform Google date-range searches without the extra step, use the FaganFinder Google interface (*http://www.faganfinder.com/engines/google.shtml*) shown in Figure 34, an alternative to the Google Advanced Search page, sporting daterange: searching via a Gregorian date pull-down menu.

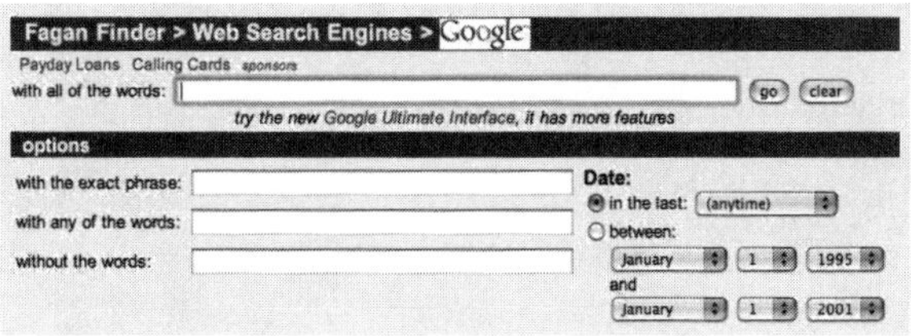

Figure 34. The FaganFinder Google interface with Gregorian-based date-range searching

More Julian dates and online computers can be found via a Google search for julian date (*http://www.google.com/search?q=julian+date*).

Index

We'd like to hear your suggestions for improving our indexes. Send email to *index@oreilly.com*.

Other Titles Available from O'Reilly

By Tara Calishain & Rael Dornfest
1st Edition March 2003
352 pages, 0-596-00447-8

By Paul Bausch
1st Edition August 2003
304 pages, 0-596-00542-3

By Rael Dornfest & Kevin Hemenway
1st Edition March 2003
432 pages, 0-596-00460-5

O'REILLY®

To order: 800-998-9938 • order@oreilly.com • www.oreilly.com
Online editions of most O'Reilly titles are available by subscription at safari.oreilly.com
Also available at most retail and online bookstores.

Other Titles Available from O'Reilly

By David A. Karp
1st Edition August 2003
352 pages, 0-596-00564-4

By Rob Flickenger
1st Edition September 2003
304 pages, 0-596-00559-8

By Raffi Krikorian
1st Edition August 2003
288 pages, 0-596-00553-9